MARCO POLO

RHODES

with Local Tips

The author's special recommendations are highlighted in yellow throughout this guide

There are five symbols to help you find your way around this guide:

Marco Polo's top recommendations – the best in each category

sites with a scenic view

places where the local people meet

places where young people get together

(102/A1)
pages and coordinates for the Road Atlas of Rhodes
(U/A1) *coordinates for the City Map of Rhodes inside back cover*
For your orientation even places that are not marked in the Road Atlas are provided with coordinates.

This travel guide was written by Christine Tsolodimos, who lived in Greece for many years, and the Greece connoisseur Klaus Bötig.

MARCO POLO

Travel guides and language guides in this series:

Alaska • Algarve • Amsterdam • Australia/Sydney • Bahamas • Barbados Barcelona • Berlin • Brittany • Brussels • California • Canada • Channel Islands Chicago and the Great Lakes • Copenhagen • Costa Brava/Barcelona Costa del Sol/Granada • Crete • Cuba • Cyprus • Dominican Republic Eastern Canada • Eastern USA • Egypt • Florence • Florida • French Riviera Gran Canaria • Greek Islands/Aegean • Hong Kong • Ibiza/Formentera Ireland • Israel • Istanbul • Italian Riviera • Jamaica • Lanzarote • London Los Angeles • Madeira • Mallorca • Malta • Menorca • Mexico • Netherlands New York • New Zealand • Normandy • Norway • Paris • Portugal • Prague Rhodes • Rocky Mountains • Rome • San Francisco • Scotland • South Africa • Southwestern USA • Switzerland • Tenerife • Thailand • Turkish Coast • Tuscany • USA: New England • USA: Southern States • Venice Washington D.C. •Western Canada • Western USA

French • German • Italian • Spanish

Marco Polo would be very interested to hear your comments and suggestions. Please write to:

North America:
Marco Polo North America
70 Bloor Street East
Oshawa, Ontario, Canada
(B) 905-436-2525

United Kingdom:
GeoCenter International Ltd
The Viables Centre
Harrow Way
Basingstoke, Hants RG22 4BJ

Cover photograph: Harbour and Palace of the Grand Masters in the city of Rhodos (Kiedrowski)
Photos: author (74, 79); O. Baumli (12, 24, 41, 42, 59); K. Bötig (70, 84);
Mauritius: Bartel (10, 53, 56, 77, 86, 89), Edmanson (9), Hubatka (101), Pigneter (68), Rawi (28),
Spectrum (55); T. Stankiewicz (4, 18, 36, 51, 62, 65); O. Suren (61); Touristik-Marketing (32, 35);
Transglobe: Sommer (22)

2nd revised edition 2001

Translator: Moll & Squire
English edition 2001: Gaia Text, Munich
Editorial director: Ferdinand Ranft
Chief editor: Marion Zorn
Cartography for the Road Atlas: © Mairs Geographischer Verlag
Design and layout: Thienhaus/Wippermann
Printed in Germany

CONTENTS

Discover Rhodes!

Variety is the spice of the island: beaches and forests, hurly-burly and solitude, temples and mosques – Rhodes has it all!

Rhodes is home to the sun. When Zeus the ancient mythological father of all gods divided the earth among the gods, Helios, the sun god, was away on his daily celestial journey and went empty-handed. He complained to Zeus, who then made an island appear out of the sea and gave it to him as a gift. Rhodes was this island. It's no wonder that the sun makes frequent appearances here, on Greece's fourth largest island. According to statistics, the sun shines 270 days of the year. Since the sun isn't afire in winter, however, there's still plenty of precipitation to make Rhodes a green island. Many hills are covered with woodlands and grapevines; olive and orange trees flourish.

In terms of economics, tourism has admittedly become far more important than agriculture. With the exception of Crete, none of the some 100 inhabited islands hosts more foreign visitors than Rhodes, 1,400 sq km in size. Nevertheless, not all the beaches have been completely built up yet. Since tourism tends to be concentrated on the coastal regions, the old Rhodes continues to live on in the many mountain and inland villages.

Rhodes (Ródos in Greek) is also the name of the "capital" city of the island. Approximately 43,500 people live in the administrative centre of the Dodecanese group of islands, which include 19 permanently inhabited islands. Many contrasts shape this lively metropolis. An old town with monuments from three millenniums (yet which is anything but a museum) is surrounded by expanding concrete; cosy speciality restaurants next to fast-food joints, the uniformity of tourism juxtaposed with the quintessence of Greek culture – the city of Rhodes offers all this in a small space. This city, even though it has so often fallen

Fortress overlooking the village and inlet of Líndos

History at a glance

3000 BC
Neolithic Period. First settlements on Rhodes

1500 BC
Mycenaean sailors settle on the island

1000–500 BC
Founding of the three Doric City States of Líndos, Kámiros and Lalyssós

490 BC
Rhodes is Persian rule

408 BC
The island is devastated by the Athenians. The three City States unite to found the city of Rhodes

304 BC
Demétrios Poliorkétes, a Macedonian general, besieges the city without success

164 BC
Rhodes becomes Roman

AD 395
After the division of the Roman Empire, Rhodes falls to the East Roman Empire. In the Byzantine Era, the island is repeatedly conquered by the Persians and Saracens, among others

1309–1522
The island falls under the rule of the Order of the Knights of St John of Jerusalem

1522
Sultan Süleyman "the Magnificent" occupies Rhodes. The island remains Turkish for nearly 400 years. Greece's struggle for independence begins in 1821

1912
The Italians conquer the Turks and occupy the island

11 September 1943
Rhodes is occupied by the Germans. Some 2,000 Jews are deported to German concentration camps. Most of them are murdered there

1945
England liberates the island

10 February 1947
Paris Peace Treaty; the Dodecanese islands become part of Greece

1967–1974
Military dictatorship. After a dubious referendum, the monarchy is abolished in 1972

1975
Another vote is taken on Greece's form of government; the majority decides in favour of a presidential democracy

1981
Greece becomes a full member of the EC. In October, a socialist government comes to power for the first time

1988
Following the EC summit in the city of Rhodes, each head of government is appointed to be an honorary citizen of a Dodecanese Island. Rhodes appoints François Mitterrand

2000
A parliament election in April confirms the majority of reigning socialists under Kostas Simitis

prey to commerce (the locals) and consumers (the tourists), is described in detail in this book because you simply can't miss the city of Rhodes.

For most holidaymakers, this is true in all senses. They remain in city of Rhodes and cling to its immediate surroundings, which presently extends to Faliráki on the east coast and Paradíssi (airport) on the west coast. They choose to spend their vacation there in the same way they could spend it at any holiday resort in the sunny south. Rhodes, an island that is more truly "Greek" than many others, shows its true character only after a second or third look.

In 1947, the Dodecanese Islands and, along with it, Rhodes, became Greek – only about a half-century, just two generations, ago. Before that, there had been 400 years of Turkish occupation, after which, for more than 40 years, the island was under Italian control. And then yet another invasion, only this time a peaceful one: sun-worshippers and educational travellers arrived, sporadically at first and then en masse. Particularly the young people of Rhodes no doubt feel torn between the different cultures.

Hardly any other Greek provincial town boasts such a selection of consumer goods and cultural and leisure amenities. The latest trends from major international fashion houses appear as quickly in Rhodes as they do in major international metropolises. Although Rhodes no longer enjoys the tax benefits it was granted in its first decades after unification with its Greek mother country, for many Greeks it is still a relatively inexpensive shopping paradise. The people of Rhodes themselves are cosmopolitan. They don't leave the many ethnic restaurants for the holidaymakers alone; they eat there themselves – a rarity in other areas of Greece.

Rhodes has so many faces and offers so many opportunities that you can do something new every day. When you've had enough of the crowded beaches in the north, with its surfboard and paddle boat rentals, beach bars and waterskiing, just drive a little to the south. It might get more barren as you go farther, but the scenery gets more and more interesting and at the same time you'll meet fewer strangers. With a little luck, you'll discover your own secluded length of beach on the southwestern coast.

On the whole, the paths tread upon by tourists run along the 220-km-long coast. The interior of the island has hardly been explored – or has been "spared" as many would put it. This is a shame only in the sense that there's nothing that keeps the locals staying in the remote, often admittedly colourless villages. Many places could benefit from a skilled and careful tourism manager breathing new life into the houses, before the last inhabitant has left. For the last 15 years, however, thanks to holidaymakers, the number of

residents on Rhodes has continued to grow. The inland villages, however, hardly benefit from this development, which is not very typical for this Greek province. They continue to die out.

Rhodes has a different face in each direction. The north offers big-city life, culture, entertainment and hurly-burly on the seashore. In the east, sandy beaches and up-and-coming holiday resorts with pleasant hotels and bungalow complexes nestling in the scenery compete with Faliráki. And, of course, there's also the (unfortunately) notoriously overcrowded, picturesque Líndos. In the west, rocky, pebbly beaches give way to sandy ones, with rougher coasts, heavy winds and surfing resorts. On the west coast, you can discover Kámiros, an ancient city located on an exceptionally beautiful area above the coast. Last, but certainly not least, it's in its southern regions that Rhodes presents itself as a typical Aegean island: barren, uninviting and almost scorching in the summer. But tourists continue to flock there anyway. Prassoníssi, the wide, sandy beach on the southernmost point of the island has been accessible via a paved road since 1999. At long last, there's a surf station, taverns and rooms to let in this windsurfing paradise.

North, south, east, west, – four variations on the same theme on the island of Rhodes. If you miss out on one of the variations, you haven't experienced the whole. The island is small enough to visit all four areas in one day. You can slowly "work through" one after another, and if you have a car, you can drive back and forth between them. The morning could be spent in the old town in the city of Rhodes, the afternoon at the beach in Prassoníssi and in the evening a stop for supper in Líndos on the way back!

Rhodes is a travel destination for anyone who isn't a big fan of beach life and swimming. The mild, wet winters result in a wide variety of flora – 29 plant species are endemic exclusively to Rhodes. About a third of the island is covered with forests – an unusually high percentage for a Greek island.

There's also an unusually large number of churches, monasteries, convents and mosques on the island. Several of these originate from the Byzantine era and at least 30 are of art-historical interest – mostly because of their frescoes or precious icons. Many of these houses of God have been built in very beautiful spots, which alone makes the trip worthwhile. Today, more and more abandoned monasteries and convents have once again become home to monks and nuns and definitely merit making a side trip. Many visitors take this opportunity to spend the night in solitude (some for the first time in their lives) with the rustling of trees, chirping cicadas and the bark of a dog. In many ways, Rhodes is still an undiscovered island.

If it's pubs and discos that you're interested in, there's plenty to go around in the city

of Rhodes. Elsewhere, in Líndos for instance, it's only outside the residential areas that anything happens after midnight. Everywhere else, the music stops and you can only have a chat at the bar. The locals have asserted their right to get a couple of hours sleep even during the tourist season, which lasts from April to October. Otherwise, they would hardly be able to get through their 12-hour-long (often longer), seven-days-a-week work week.

At the beginning of December, after the last tourist has flown home, a great calm after the storm sets in: chairs are brought in, windows are nailed down, the door key is turned. Now it's time for winter. Some people from Rhodes take advantage of this time to become tourists themselves and take one- or two-month holidays to Europe. The *kamákia*, the Rhodesian counterpart of Italian Papagallis, take their own holidays as well. In summer, it's best just to let the spruced-up young Adonises sit in the tourist cafés. There are plenty of other opportunities to get to know the pleasant, friendly people on Rhodes. Owners of small guest houses, shopkeepers, weavers in Archángelos or Afántou… Anyone who is looking for a conversation – in English, with a few Greek words thrown in, or even in sign language – will discover, especially away from the large tourist spots, that there's one thing that the people of Rhodes didn't forget: there is only one word in standard Greek for both "stranger" and "guest". This word, *filoxenía*, which means hospitality, implies friendliness towards strangers. This is particularly true during festivals, and the memory of a *panij'ri*, a festival held in honour of the patron saint of a town church, is one of the nicest souvenirs of Rhodes that you can take back home with you.

The history, people and cultures of Rhodes have blended together since ancient times

Not to forget, side trips to neighbouring islands can be taken from Rhodes. Excursion boats depart daily for trips to the former sponge-fishing and shipyard island of Sími. You can take a fast hydrofoil boat to the more distant Kos, once home to the famous doctor Hippocrates, and small propeller planes fly to the rugged island of Kárpathos. You can even take a day trip by ship to neighbouring Turkey if you'd like.

From Aleppo pines to távli players

The people and island of Rhodes: a miniature universe of its own

Architecture

Only a few ancient Greek buildings have survived. Above all, Líndos and Kámiros attest to the earlier wealth of the island. The foreign rulers – the Knights of St John of Jerusalem, the Turks, the Italians – have all left their mark on Rhodes. The Knights Road in the city of Rhodes, lined by buildings in late Gothic style, could just as easily be found in Avignon or Florence. The domes of the mosques built during Turkish rule give the old town a touch of the Orient. The imposing buildings on the shore road, the ornate aquarium and the playful Kallithéa thermal baths are the work of Italian architects.

The traditional Rhodes family house consists of one room with a loft. The family would sleep upstairs, whereas animals were left downstairs for the night.

Like a theatre set: the walls and towers of the reconstructed Palace of the Grand Masters in the city of Rhodes

Population

Statistics had already predicted the trend in the 1950s: the population of the Greek province was and is diminishing. People are moving into the city or going abroad in search of training, education and work. As a result, more than half of all Greeks live in Athens and Thessaloniki. One-third of all Greek citizens live in foreign countries; many families have been living abroad for several generations.

Depite this trend, the population of Rhodes has been rising sharply since about 1970. There were approximately 66,000 people living there in 1971; today, about 100,000 people are permanent residents of the island. Roughly half of these live in the city of Rhodes, some 17,000 in the municipality of Ialyssós and the rest in the island's 41 villages. Most of the people are Greek and belong to the Greek Orthodox Church. There are still around 2,000 Muslims of Turkish descent with their own religious leader.

The island's renewed growth is due to the tourism that has

It's easier to climb the steep path from Líndos to the acropolis on a mule

boomed continually, sometimes explosively, since the 1970s. Only about 20 per cent of the money earned on Rhodes derives from such sources of revenue as agriculture or weaving. There are more than 500 hotels on the island, with over 75,000 beds. And they are rarely empty. More than 300,000 holidaymakers from the UK and Germany alone visit Rhodes every year. Time and again, it happens that some do not want to return home. Some 2,000 Scandinavians and about 800 people from German-speaking countries have taken up residence on Rhodes, and most of them make a living from tourism.

Fauna

Donkeys, mules and goats, the typical working animals of the Mediterranean region, are characteristic of Rhodes as well. Songbirds are traditional pets in Greece: domestic finches, canaries and especially colourful parrots are among the favourites on Rhodes. Dogs are usually kept as watchdogs while homeless cats stretch out in sunny doorways and on rocking fishing boats. The larger mammals of the island include weasels, martens, foxes and badgers, but you can rarely catch sight of them, in contrast to the 70 fallow deer on the island. Stag and doe are the heraldic animals of Rhodes. These animals all live both in the wild as well as in a 70,000 sq m open area in Rodíni Park.

There's a very wide variety of insects and butterflies in Rhodes. The butterflies in Petaloúdes valley, however, increasingly try to escape from the noisy visitors. You are therefore more likely to see them mounted behind glass than in the wild. There is also a large brown-grey species of lizard called *sáwra*. Sometimes on summer evenings, you can see flesh-coloured, nearly transparent geckos sitting beneath

lights, almost glued to the wall – moving only if an insect comes within their reach or they are frightened away by noise. You may encounter some snakes on a mountain hike, but they are, for the most part, harmless.

Sadly, the fish population throughout Greece is declining. For decades, schools of fish have been decimated by dynamite-fishing and increased pollution of the sea plays a role in their decline as well. In addition, many fishermen do not accurately follow the regulated fishing seasons and, for example, catch small *marídes* (whitefish) before their first spawning because they supposedly taste better. In many Greek holiday resorts, fish must be imported during the peak season to meet the demand. One consolation: there's still a large selection of fish in Mandráki Harbour.

Flora

Rhodes is a botanical treasure trove: 29 species of plant are endemic exclusively to Rhodes. In contrast to most of the Aegean islands, Rhodes is very green, despite having suffered several devastating forest fires in the past. In the north and in the interior, there are still many forests with Italian cypresses and Aleppo pines. You'll also find sweet chestnuts and date palms here.

The many different prickly shrubs entangled in one another on the mountain slopes and dry flatlands are typical of Greek islands, as are; Juniper, broom and mastic, as well as many almost-intoxicating, fragrant herbs (oregano, thyme, lavender). The keen cook can either buy these herbs and spices to fill his or her spice rack, or can collect them for free while hiking in the mountains. In spring, the island becomes a carpet of flowers: red corn poppies, yellow clover and purple cyclamen in the forests, red blossoms of pomegranate trees and small Rhodian peonies everywhere. Roses in the true sense of the word are hard to find on Rhodes, the "island of roses"!

You can sit and watch citrus fruits and clusters of grapes grow and ripen before your very eyes. However, the farmers harvest fruit and vegetables only for local consumption.

Women

In the villages, you can still sometimes see a Greek patriarch riding on a mule while his wife trails behind, heavily loaded down with brushwood. And it's always the men who sit and blab on in the *kafeníon* while the women cook the meals, take care of the children, do the housework and tend to the animals. Even today, Greece remains a male-dominated society. Tourism on Rhodes has not greatly affected the centuries-old patriarchal traditions.

The first son of a couple is christened with the paternal name of the grandfather; the first daughter with the name of the paternal grandmother. The maternal grandparent names are given only starting with the second daughter and/or second son. This cus-

tom explains why there are relatively few first names in Greece – most couples maintain this tradition even today. To avoid mix-ups, the father's name is used as a second Christian name on official documents. Women generally use their last names in the genitive form: the wife and daughters of Mr Argirós are thus called Argiroú, "of Argirós".

If Eléni Argiroú marries a Mr Chrístos Saríkas, her ID would read "Eléni Chrístos Saríkas", which in essence means "Eléni, owned by Chrístos Saríkas". Eléni has, at least on paper, simply changed the name of her owner. This is not taken literally today, particularly since women are permitted to keep their maiden name after marriage. However, this usage of language is indeed a reflection of the position of women.

Greece – a land of machos? Perhaps. The following example is proof thereof: Maria, aged 19, must return with her parents to her unfamiliar hometown of Líndos "in order to marry a decent man from our island and not get any ideas over there". In the eyes of her family, she doesn't need any more vocational or professional training. One year later, she is married to the young man from Líndos who was chosen by her parents.

And now an example that proves the opposite: Tsambíka, aged 23, is from a village on the west coast. She has been living in the city of Rhodes since her secondary school days, and both her younger sisters have moved there as well. After having taken her final exams at school, Tsambíka completed her training as a tour guide. She speaks fluent German, English and French. Marriage? Maybe later.

In general, young Greek women have less freedom than their contemporaries in other European countries. It's normal for teenagers to have sexual relations, but, for the most part, the parents of the girl know nothing about it, or at least pretend not to. A woman should be a virgin on her wedding night while the husband should be as sexually experienced as possible – a bizarre double-standard.

Geography and geology

Rhodes covers an area of approximately 1,400 sq km and is the fourth-largest Greek island. It looks like a rhombus that has been tipped to the right and compressed, and flattened in some places. It is 78 km from north-east to south-west and, at its widest point, 38 km of land separate the west and east coasts. The entire coast is 220 km long.

Rhodes is much closer to Turkey than to the Greek mainland. The Turkish coast is about 20 km from the city of Rhodes.

Most of the island is made up of limestone, sandstone and hornstone, most of which is between 25 and 40 million years old. At 1,215 m, the highest mountain is Mt. Atáviros in the west. The delicious spring water of the same name comes from here and is sold as bottled water.

The city of Rhodes is the capital of the Greek province Dodekínissos, "the twelve islands". In reality, however, there are 200 islands and islets, of which only about 20 are inhabited. Together, they make up an area covering some 2,700 sq km and have fewer than 200,000 residents.

Greek coffee

For centuries, the black mud in the white mini-demitasse has correctly been called Turkish coffee, since the method of preparation originated from Turkey. In the 1970s a coffee company conducted a massive (by Greek standards) advertising campaign to rename the coffee.

To prepare the coffee, you need finely ground, light-brown mocha, sugar, a special pot (made from aluminium, brass or copper) with a long handle called a *bríki*, a spoon, water, a small gas burner and some talent. The water, coffee and sugar are brought to a boil – one spoonful of each for a *métrio* (medium strength and sweetness). Connoisseurs maintain that there are numerous variations. Besides *métrio*, beginners should remember the difference between the terms *skétos* (black), *glikós* (sweet) and *varíglikos* (sweet and strong). Whether the mixture is first stirred in the *bríki* and then set upon the flame or whether boiling the mixture twice really refines the taste is a matter of preference – opinions vary on the point.

Kamáki

Kamáki means "harpoon" and, in colloquial Greek, "harpoon-making" means picking up women. The *kamáki* (plural: *kamákia)* is the equivalent of the Italian *papagallo*. They usually wear long trousers with razor-sharp creases or trendy jeans and spotless shoes. A crisp shirt in this season's colours and a gold chain with a cross worn on a half-bare hairy chest complete the out-fit. The *kamákia* sit in sidewalk cafés and surveil their prey, as described in a Greek pop song: "Two young men sit in a café, each one sprawled across three chairs. It's cool under the awning. They have cast out their net: Do you like Greece, Miss? What are you doing this evening? Do you like, Mademoiselle, the Greece?" (If you want to know how the song continues, you can find the song "Do you like the Greek?" on the CD titled *Made in Greece*. Music by Arjíris Kounádis, sung by Antónis Kalojánnis.)

These Rhodian Adonises are considered to be the champions of the Greek "harpoons". Only local girls are safe from them because their "virtue" is still guarded by strict fathers, brothers and uncles.

Climate

Most tempting in April and May, when the island is covered in lush green and the temperature doesn't exceed 25°C (77°F) during the day. You can swim from mid-April until the beginning of November. It rains a lot on Rhodes during the winter, sometimes so heavily that in the villages, school is cancelled because water has to be drained from the class-rooms before the

students can return. For the most part, however, these cloudbursts last only a short time.

During the hot months of July and August, the thermometer can reach up to 33°C (91°F) in the shade. This is actually a tolerable temperature by Greek standards, thanks to the cool, frequently strong north-westerly wind, the Meltémi, that blows on Rhodes almost the whole summer long.

The Colossus of Rhodes

It was one of the seven wonders of the ancient world and was cast in bronze by Chares of Líndos between 294 and 282 BC. Fifty years later, it was destroyed in an earthquake. The statue of Helios, the sun god, was supposedly 33 m high. Unfortunately, we don't know what it looked like. Most likely, however, the Colossus did not stand with its legs straddled over the harbour entrance as tradition has long maintained.

Literature

Two books are especially recommendable as holiday reading during a stay on Rhodes. Lawrence Durrell, the well-known British novelist, vividly describes his experiences on Rhodes shortly after the end of the war in his book *Reflections on a Marine Venus: A Companion to the Landscape of Rhodes*. The history of the Order of the Knights of St John of Jerusalem is chronicled by Ernle Bradford in his accessibly written *The Shield and the Sword*.

Military

In Greece, a man is still not considered to be a real man unless he has served as a soldier. Recruits still have to endure hazing reminiscent of mediaeval times. The pay (980 Dr a month) is not even enough for two packs of Cowboy cigarettes. Conscientious objectors have had vested rights only since 1997. Alternative community service (in lieu of military service) is unattractive, however, and is twice as long in duration (even though it was shortened from 24 months to 18 months in the late 1980s). Most recruits must fulfil their basic training far away from home. Soldiers are stationed on Rhodes as well.

Music and dance

While you're visiting Rhodes, you'll hear the music that is currently popular throughout Greece. At festivals, typical traditional Greek island music is played (important instruments include the violin and the *iagoúto*, a large string instrument with a large resonance chamber, which is played with a long plectrum).

Since the movie *Zorba the Greek* was shown worldwide, people everywhere know how much the Greek people like to dance – and how good they are at it. On a Greek theme evening arranged by the tour operators, holidaymakers make an attempt at Greek dancing, they put their arms around each other's shoulders and try to match the first steps of the Syrtáki with its famous melody. The Syrtáki is nothing more than a simpler version (created only for the film) of the classic Chassápiko, whose steps and patterns cannot

In the spirit of Marco Polo

Marco Polo was the first true world traveller. He travelled with peaceful intentions forging links between the East and the West. His aim was to discover the world, and explore different cultures and environments without changing or disrupting them. He is an excellent role model for the travellers of today and the future. Wherever we travel we should show respect for other peoples and the natural world.

be learnt in just one Rhodes holiday.

There are traditional round dances, both for men and for women. The Tsámikos, with its heavy stomping steps, originates from the mountainous areas of the country; men and women on the islands dance the Syrtós together, while couples dance the carefree happy Bállos.

For a couple of years, the traditional music has been experiencing a renaissance. Even in discos, the Zeibékiko is played sometimes, a slow solo dance that doesn't have any structured steps and is considered to be the king of all Greek dances. It was Míkis Theodoràkis who first introduced Greek music to foreign countries; later the film *Rembetica* (Rembétiko) featured the music style that is often referred to as Greek blues: the simple lyrics speak of love, poverty, hard work and escape through drinking. Important solo instruments include the *bouzoúki* (a string instrument) and its smaller relative, the *baglamás*. For decades, listening to Rembétiko music was frowned upon. In the 1960s,the composer Mános Chatzidákis (*Never on Sundays*) made a few classic pieces socially acceptable by performing new versions of them.

There is a very lively singer-songwriter, Chanson and pop music scene in Greece. The first impressions of these are conveyed by the offerings in the music pubs in the Old Town of Rhodes city.

Nature and environmental conservation

Most Greek people are still not very environmentally conscious in the way they treat the land, water and air. There's always enough to go around, the island will always be renewed after the winter storms and the ocean will be left unspoilt. In the meantime, Greece does have a "green" party and has representation of several recognized environmentalist groups, such as the WWF and Greenpeace, however the environmentalists' warnings and demands are just voices crying in the wilderness. Consumption and disposal is the order of the day. Plastic, disposable packaging and cleaning agents inundate the country and pile up into huge mountains of rubbish. In some cities,

people are beginning to sort rubbish and recycle it as much as possible. Aluminium is now being recycled on Rhodes. Unfortunately, recycling bins for cans are not found everywhere. People take the shortest routes by car and leave (mostly unfiltered) clouds of exhaust fumes behind. However, many critics forget that the "good old" but difficult times were not too long ago in Greece and the knowledge that new comforts have their price is slow in coming.

In terms of using alternative energy, however, Greece is far ahead of most of the rest of Europe. The state offers tax incentives to lure people into installing solar panels and more and more homeowners are jumping at the opportunity to do so – less for the sake of the environment than for the money they can save on electricity bills. Windmills, the traditional energy source of the Greek islands, are found on the west coast of Rhodes, where it's always very windy. A hotel and potter's workshop have recently started operating wind power plants.

Drinking water is becoming scarcer and scarcer with each passing year because the ground water reserves are running low. Today, Rhodes's neighbouring islands, Chálki and Sími, already have to "import" water in tankers. Therefore, everyone should use this precious liquid sparingly.

Orthodox church services

Almost all Greeks belong to the Greek Orthodox Church. They

Greek priest

see themselves as apostles and closely connected to early Christians, since their principles of faith haven't changed very much since the ninth century. Orthodox church services frequently last two or three hours. However, only a few churchgoers hold out for such a long service. There are continual comings and goings and people occasionally converse with each other during services. Sermons are rare. The main feature of the service is the responsory of the daily-changing liturgy which is celebrated by the priest and some of the laypersons. There are no hymnbooks.

Education

If you visit Greece often and at different times of the year, you might get the impression that Greek children don't attend school at all. School is out for vacation in July, August, and in September as well. It's closed for Christmas and Easter, of

course. The school gates are closed at least four months of the year. Some might say that you can consider this as fortunate, since the Greek national school system is agony for all involved: rotting buildings, poorly trained and underpaid teachers, as well as alternating morning and afternoon classes due to an insufficient number of classrooms. In addition, there is a labyrinth of passing and examination regulations that is meddled with by each new education minister.

The big winners are the private afternoon and evening schools (you can recognize them by the name *frontistírio* on their signs), which offer expensive supplementary lessons to prepare pupils for annual final exams. Without the *frontistírio*, applicants hardly have a chance at the admission procedures of the university. These crash courses take place during school holidays, of course, effectively reducing school-free time for middle-school pupils and senior classes down to two months a year. Another problem on Rhodes is that many villages don't even have their own schools and continuing school education is only available in the island's capital city.

Sports

You can swim almost anywhere; the prettiest places are the beaches on the east coast. The strong winds of the west coast are great for windsurfing. Surfing schools can be found in the large hotels of Ixía and Faliráki. If you want to try your hand at steering a pedal boat or motorboat, or go water-skiing, you'll find plenty of opportunities to do so. In the city of Rhodes, you can even rent sailboats fit for competition.

Fishing is permitted everywhere. Supposedly, the most fish take the bait in Kallithéa, Líndos, Gennádi and Kámiros. You're allowed only to harpoon fish that weigh more than 150 g.

Scubadiving is allowed only if accompanied by a local diving instructor. This is to prevent holidaymakers from taking ancient art treasures that are still laying undiscovered on the bottom of the sea. A golf course (18 holes) is located at Afántou and a great number of tennis courts are available.

Above all, the most popular sports on Rhodes are basketball and football (Diagóras Rhódou, the football club in the city of Rhodes, was in the first national league).

Language

Only since 1948 modern Greek has been the official language of Rhodes. Older people still speak a lot of Italian – a fallback to occupation times – and English and German can at least be understood most everywhere. In the city of Rhodes and in Líndos, it's quite possible that a waiter in a restaurant will approach a table with two menus in hand – perhaps one in English and one in Greek, or one in German and one in French. The Greek you may have learnt before your holidays naturally goes unused.

The thing that keeps throwing you off is transcribing the

Greek alphabet into Latin letters. What is it then? Péfkos, Péfki or maybe Péfka? Sgouroú or Asgouróu? Thárri, Thári or Thórdi? Some places on Rhodes have almost as many different names as there are maps of the island. This is also owing to the Greek "bilingualism". In addition to the modern Greek language, which contains Italian and Turkish elements and is interspersed with many English and French words, there is also a standard language which is much closer to ancient Greek in terms of vocabulary and grammar.

In the past, legal decrees, judgements and other official documents were written exclusively in standard Greek. It is still spoken in churches today. Officially, standard Greek has been abolished, but much of it still remains, for example in names of places. On top of all this comes the difficult spelling and the peculiarity that many nouns in the Greek language have more than one gender. An example: the holiday village south of Líndos is named after the pines that flourish there. In Greek, the word "pine" can be *péfkos, péfko* or *péfki*. Plural versions of the word are *péfka* and *péfki* (written differently). It's almost a wonder, then, that the place has only three names and not five. In this book, we'll stick to the version used most often. Our readers should not be put off by Greek spelling, such as the five i-sounds that are all pronounced the same way but written differently. Whether there is an *ei*, an *oi*, an *i* or a *y* – we consistently use an *i*, unless the word is already internationally known as being spelled in a certain way. In order to make pronunciation easier to understand, we use our method of transcription to try to come as close as possible to the spoken word, and place an accent mark on the stressed syllable of the word. However, don't forget that the accentuation of many place names can change. Nevertheless, chin up! You can always find someone on Rhodes to show you the way – even without speaking perfect Greek!

Strikes

If the letter you wrote home is still on its way three weeks later, if the Olympic Airways flight to Crete is cancelled, if there's a sign on the bank that says *closed all day* – then it is strike time again. Everything is at a standstill … Greece experiences one or two waves of strikes every year. It's not surprising since wages and salaries chronically lag behind inflation and the annual "automatic inflationary adjustment" is at best just a drop in the ocean. But don't worry, labour disputes are conducted far less aggressively in holiday areas. There's always a bank or exchange booth open, and a flight home with a foreign charter company is guaranteed. A taxi driver will gladly interrupt a strike for a worthwhile trip. If there's a postal strike, however, it's probably best to deliver your holiday postcards in person after you return home.

Távli

Two men at a table, a backgammon board with two dice and thick, round plastic playing pieces between them, heads are lowered, all muscles are tense – please do not disturb! *Távli* is much more than just a Greek version of backgammon. *Távli* is as much a part of life for a traditional Greek man as mother, military service and strong mocha coffee in the morning. It's played in the *kafeníon* or at home, for example on Sunday afternoons when the women are having a rest and the children are napping. Deserted streets, closed blinds and the clacking sounds heard on the balconies means afternoon quiet time, *távli* time. Experts can play (at least) three variations: *plakotó* (roughly translated as "bang the board"), *févga* (get lost) and *pórtes* (doors). For many, *távli* is a form of both, relaxation and communication. The men chat about this, that and the other thing (a favourite: politics). Winning is irrelevant. There are, however, obsessed *távli* players who defeat their partners with the first roll of the dice, who throw their playing pieces on the board amid martial threats of, "I'm gonna show you who's boss! I'll tear you to pieces!" If two of this type meet up, the backgammon board is sure to get broken.

Election Sundays

In Greece, most museums and archaeological sites are closed on election day. As soon as the polling places are closed, no alcohol can officially be sold for the rest of the day. This is supposed to prevent already quick-tempered persons from becoming even more upset.

Forest fires

"Protect the Forests", "Caution: Danger of Forest Fires" – signs like these are placed on roadsides with good reason. Year after year, Greece suffers from disastrous forest fires, primarily in August when the hot sun shines mercilessly. It's not just the proverbial tossed-away match that's to blame; fires are also helped along by land speculators and terrorists. Unfortunately, Rhodes is not spared from the fires. In recent years, several places in the centre and southern parts of the island have been burnt. Fortunately, important tourism areas were not affected. Newly effected, strict safety measures should help to avoid new catastrophes. It is prohibited to enter any forest between the hours of 9.30 pm and 5.30 am.

Hiking

Do you like walking? If you're a good walker, you can see many parts of the island that are unknown even to the locals and maybe you will discover some scenic treasures, for example, on the slopes of Mt. Atáviros, on Profíis Ilás, or around the area of Láerma. Sturdy hiking boots, long pants, something to cover your head, plenty of water and some strong sunscreen are necessities if you plan to set off on a long hike. And, remember, you should never hike alone.

Ippotes Bar

Chatting between cheese and pears

Olive oil, lots of herbs and spices and plenty of conversation are essential ingredients of Greek cuisine

Food

Anything you can order to eat at a Greek restaurant in your hometown, you can get in Rhodes. The cuisine of Rhodes is essentially Greek cuisine – strongly influenced by neighbouring Turkey. You can see this influence in the names of many dishes. For example, stuffed grape leaves, a popular starter, are called *dolmádes*, but the word certainly isn't purely Greek. Of course, you could always order the dish in Greek – *ampelófilla* – but this is very rarely used.

Or, to keep with starters, take *tzatzíki*, as an example. This yoghurt dish (yoghurt mixed with finely cut or grated cucumbers and garlic) is called *cacík* in Turkish and these neighbours most likely have original rights to the word. A word of caution, however: discussing the Greek or Turkish origin of a recipe, word or piece of music can put many Greeks in a bad mood – a holdover from 400 years of Turkish rule.

After all that sightseeing, you deserve a refreshing snack

Olive oil, onions, garlic and strong spices, such as oregano and caraway, are the basics of Greek cuisine. A bounty of regional vegetables, such as aubergine, courgettes and okra, are also staples in Greece. Many tourists must develop a taste for mutton and goat meat, something that comes with time.

A complete Greek supper begins with *mezédes* (starters). There is usually a large selection to choose from: fried aubergine *(melitzánes)* or courgettes *(kolokíthia)*, fish roe salad *(taramosaláta)*, pasties filled with feta cheese, spinach or both *(tirópita, spanakópita, spanakotirópita)*, anchovies *(antzoújies)*, giant haricot beans *(jígantes)* … You order a starter and a little while later, the table is full of food. Everyone eats from a shared plate, but don't eat too much so that you save room for the main course. You don't really "eat" the high-

calorie *mezédes,* rather you "pick" from it.

Traditional main courses are: *jemistés* (baked vegetables, usually tomatoes or green bell peppers, stuffed with rice and/or minced meat); *biftéki* (meatballs, sometimes stuffed with cheese); *pastítsio* (baked macaroni and minced meat); *stifádo* (stewed beef or rabbit), *brizóla moscharísia* or *brizóla chiriní* (pork chops or beef cutlets), *arní sto foúrno* (roast mutton, ususally served with potatoes); *paidákia* (lamb chops), *bakaliáros* (dried cod, soaked in water and fried) served with *skorádaliá* (mashed potatoes flavoured with garlic and olive oil). Inexpensive and delicious fish dishes include *marídes tiganités* (fried whitefish) and *xifías* (swordfish, the taste almost resembles steak). Seafood is considered a delicacy, and dishes include *barboúnia* (red barbel), *garídes* (scampi) and *astakós* (lobster). The exquisiteness of these seafood dishes is reflected accordingly in their price.

To a large extent, most restaurants and pubs have adapted to the tastes of their foreign guests. Very small orders, such as a "Greek salad and a glass of water" are filled without hesitation (unthinkable in a taverna in earlier times). Many chefs now hold back on the amount of garlic and olive oil they use in order to go easy on tourists' stomachs and to meet the demands of the dieting craze that has arrived in Greece. Vegetarian dishes are appearing on more and more menus, and, unfortunately, so are adventurous crossblends of

The ideal meal for holidays: fresh fish, a Greek salad and a glass of wine

traditional recipes, such as a swordfish shish-kebab *(xif'as soufláki).* In village tavernas, you can order a fried egg *(avgó máti)* or scrambled eggs *(avgá tiganitá)* with a Greek salad *(choriátiki saláta,* important ingredients of which are tomatoes, cucumbers, feta cheese, onions, olives and olive oil) and french-fried potatoes *(patátes tiganités)* on the side. The waiter brings bread to the table when you sit down.

Locally grown fruit is often served for dessert. In summer, chilled watermelon or honeydew melon *(karpoúzi* or *pepóni)* is delightfully refreshing. You can also order both together. The triangular pieces of red and dark yellow fruit arrive mixed together on a large platter, sometimes with ice cubes placed between them. Carmel pudding *(krem karamelé)* and yoghurt mixed with honey *(jiaoúrti me méli,* especially good in the mountain village of Siánna) are also popular dessert choices.

You can also shop for yourself and choose from the large

selection offered at supermarkets. You don't necessarily need to know the language for this. Moreover, foreign languages and sign language are understood at many markets and food shops. You can get products such as muesli or whole-grain bread, but they definitely cost more than at home.

Drinks

In a good Greek restaurant or pub, regardless of the price-range, a carafe of fresh water is brought to your table along with bread and cutlery. It's traditional to drink wine with meals. Because of its mild climate and large number of sunny days, Rhodes is a good region for vineyards. Some internationally recognise wines come from the Caïr vintners' co-operative and the Emery wine cellars. Popular wines include Ilios and Grand Maître (both dry white wines) as well as Chevalier de Rhodes (red, dry) and the more expensive Villaret (a light white wine). Sparkling wines and sweet liqueurs are also produced on Rhodes. The Greeks have copied beer drinking from the tourists. Löwenbräu, Carlsberg and Heineken are some of the internationally known brands that you can get almost everywhere.

On Rhodes, marc schnapps (*zoúma,* or *ts'pouro*, in local parlance) or the famous anise seed brandy called oúzo (often spiked with water, turning it milky-white) are served as aperitifs. Small helpings of high-calorie tidbits called *mezés* (the same name given to the starter platter) are served with aperitifs. In beach restaurants and pubs, *mezés* are often marinated or grilled octopus *(chtapódi)* or olives and cheese, anchovies or marinated bell peppers. In Greece, it's customary to eat something hearty, to "soak up the alcohol", when you're drinking.

The selection of non-alcoholic drinks varies. You can find cocktails made from freshly squeezed fruit almost anywhere, and you can buy bottled drinking water (for example, Atvíros).

There's coffee in all variations imaginable. In addition to the traditional strong mocha, there's filtered coffee, espresso, cappuccino, café au lait and instant coffee. Young people in particular like to drink "nes frappé" (cold, foamy Nescáfe coffee) – a drink, however, that shouldn't be tried by people with sensitive stomachs.

Sweets

A speciality of Greek bakers is a dry, sweet pastry intended to be dipped in coffee, *voutímatata.* Pieces are sold individually and you can mix and match different kinds. A type of apple cake called *milópita* also tastes very good. Compositions of honey, nuts and syrup, offered for example at the bakery at Mandráki Harbour, weaken the calorie-conscious.

Traditional classic sweets are *baklavás* (a type of nut pastry), *kataífi*, which looks like a croissant bound by a sugared piece of string, and *loukoumádes* (little balls of yeast dough with

honey). All three are guaranteeed to taste sweeter than you think they will. As a slightly lower-calorie alternative, try the *pásta* (tart), and if you want just a regular piece of cake, order "cake".

Restaurants and pubs

If you don't like Greek cooking, you can find international dishes on Rhodes as well. However, these frequently taste like the chef has only a vague idea of how to prepare them. For the best and often the cheapest meals, order what the locals eat. However, there's no denying that outside the city of Rhodes, its surroundings and Líndos, it's hard to find a restaurant or pub that has a pleasant atmosphere to go with the good food. For the most part, they are barrack-like buildings, hastily built because the owner wanted to secure his or her piece of the tourism pie as quickly as possible. Another problematic species of the Rhodes proprietor is the "renamer". If you eat a first-rate meal in a cosy *tavérna* and you ask the waiter to write down the (admittedly) difficult name of the establishment – when you return there next year, the name hanging over the entrance might well have been changed to "Original Greek Fish Tavern" or the like. And you can only hope that the fish tastes as good as before. Paradoxically, the Greek term for the type of restaurant or pub is written below the English name. The brief descriptions below should help orientate you a little.

Modest of a good value and often cosy, the *tavérna* can be easily recognized by its plastic or paper tablecloths, plain cutlery and small, thick wine glasses without a stem. In an *estiatório*, you can expect a larger menu, although the atmosphere is not inviting for lingering over a meal. In particular, many *estiatória* in the city specialize in serving quick lunches to working locals on their lunch breaks. The more cultivated (and more expensive) variation of the *estiatório* is called a restaurant. There you can find international dishes on the menu. The *psistariá* serves inexpensive grilled items to eat quickly or take away.

Black magic

Don't be surprised if someone puts his or her empty coffee cup upside down on the saucer. This probably means that there's a woman at the table interpreting the coffee grounds. She's predicting the future of the person who drank the coffee by reading the crevice-like patterns formed in the black layer of viscous broth that have run down the inside of the cup – and many people on Rhodes still believe in these prophecies. There are even women who earn a living by "reading coffee grounds" and performing other types of fortune-telling.

The best place to eat fish is at a *psarotavérna* near the ocean. It's hard to find a Greek equivalent to a beer pub or wine tavern. In Greece, a good glass of wine is always accompanied by a good meal or at least some *mezés.* If you just want to have a drink, the best place to go is a *kafeníon*. There, you can order mocha coffee, tea and soft drinks, sometimes an oúzo or *tsípouro* – however, these places are only for men. There is no law that prohibits Greek women from entering a *kafeníon*, but, in view of the male-dominated society, women voluntarily choose to stay away. Women prefer to drink their coffee in a *zacharoplastío*, a type of café that's also a popular meeting place for young people. The *kafé-bars*, also called *snack bars*, serve drinks, sweets and snacks, such as toasted sandwiches or mini-pizzas. The furnishings and prices sometimes recall similar places in Italy. The majority of fast-food establishments on Rhodes have Greek food on the menu, but offer poor quality at a high price.

If you want to ensure that you won't be surrounded only by fellow tourists, don't go out to lunch before 1.30 pm and plan to eat supper after 9.30 pm. In Greece, 8 pm is still considered afternoon and no one is thinking about supper. On Rhodes, a meal is not just a time to eat, but is a time to communicate with other people as well. Greeks prefer to invite new friends for a meal in a *tavérna* or restaurant rather than their homes. Contracts are negotiated and political networks are established between courses (as the phrase says "chatting between cheese and pears"), the Greek version of an American "power lunch".

Set meals are usually offered only in larger restaurants. Other than that, it's customary to share starters and then order the main course. The waiter will usually tell you about the specials of the day that aren't on the menu. If not, just ask him. One or two servings of side dishes, such as french-fried potatoes and salad, can be ordered for everyone at the table, just as with the *mezédes.* This makes the meal less expensive than ordering everything individually.

In Greece, it's normal for one person to pay for everyone – and often to refuse even symbolic contributions from the others to help pay the bill. A frequent variant is that everyone puts some money in the middle of the table until there's enough to pay the bill. It's only with considerable effort that Greek waiters have become accustomed to the fact that many foreign tourists almost always split the bill after a meal. It's best to tell the waiter when ordering how the bill will be paid later.

Restaurant opening hours

Most *tavérnas* are open from about 11 am to midnight. Only some of the finer restaurants are sometimes closed between the hours of 4 pm to 6 pm, or don't open at all until 6 pm.

COLOSSUS
RHODES
RHODES
RHODES
VISA
Bad

The sun in your pocket

Fragrant thyme, feta cheese, oúzo and brightly coloured ceramic-souvenirs of Rhodes to take back home with you

Caution, a holiday on Rhodes can be expensive! The goods offered at boutiques, jewellers and arts-and-crafts shops can just as easily be bought in most other big cities. In the city of Rhodes and Líndos, besides all the usual goods like clothing, electrical appliances and sporting goods, you'll find a large selection of luxury items, such as furs and valuable jewellery. If you're looking to buy souvenirs, there are plenty of small and large, practical and frivolous items to choose from: matchbox holders adorned with jumping dolphins, Souvláki skewers with ornately adorned handles, portable *távli* games – all the things people buy while on holiday. Be sure to shop around; it's not at all unusual to find the same item being sold much cheaper at a shop a couple of blocks down the street. Haggling over the price is done only for expensive and/or rare goods.

The most beautiful ones are in the museums, but there is still a large selection of colourful "Líndos Plates" that you can buy as souvenirs

Although the tax preferences that were introduced in 1948 to help boost the economy that had been shaken by war and occupation no longer apply, many Greeks still consider Rhodes to be a place where they can get good value for their money. For example, Scottish whiskey can be bought cheaper on Rhodes than it can be in Scotland. Eyeglass frames, as well as medicine, are cheaper than in Germany. If you want to eat, drink or smoke inexpensively, be sure to buy Greek products. Many goods are comparable to foreign brands. Quite a few tourists buy a tin of Papadópoulos chocolate-nut filled biscuits (although quite a few tins never make it all the way home!), oúzo, Mextaxá brandy or a carton of Greek cigarettes as souvenirs. A word of caution, however: the relatively cheap traditional Greek cigarette brands, such as Assos, Karélia or Santé, are almost as strong as roll-ups.

Antique replicas

Antique busts, vases, oil lamps and even Classical statues –

replicas of course – can be bought in the city of Rhodes in a national shop near the museums. Small pieces run around 3,400 Dr. Icons are offered there as well. You can find replicas of antique treasures at jewellery shops as well.

Food
If you have enough room left in your suitcase, you can take some of Rhodes with you and have a "Greek evening" at home. For example, buy some olives and olive oil (olive oil from Kalamáta is very good and available in tins); feta cheese (the heavily salted kinds will survive the plane trip); herbs and spices; pistachios; sweets and Greek mocha coffee (Bravo and other brands are packaged in aluminium foil and can be found at supermarkets, or they can be bought loose in the coffee roastery). And be sure you don't forget to pick up a special mocha coffee-pot *(bríki)*!

Ceramics
In Ancient Greece, bowls, jugs, vases and goblets from Rhodes were famous throughout the Mediterranean area. At least part of this tradition has been maintained. Potters from Rhodes have a good reputation throughout the whole of Greece. However, hand- or foot-operated potter's wheels used in ancient times have been replaced by electric ones. Nevertheless, it's worthwhile to make a visit to a potter's workshop and see the pottery in all its different phases of production. A speciality of Rhodes: colourful painted plates to use as wall hangings.

Clothing
You can find everything in Rhodes that is found in other big cities, and often for less money than you'd pay at home, on account of the good exchange rate. There are also tailors who will have your shirt, trousers or even an entire suit ready in a couple of days.

Kombolóia
The *kombolói* is the most typical accessory, especially for older Greeks. It resembles a rosary, but no longer has any religious significance. Greeks sit in the *kafeníon*, run the pearls through their fingers while mumbling; some sharp-tongued people might say they repeat the same words over and over: "I have a lot to do, I have so much to do, I have a lot to do ..." *Kombolóia* can be found in every design imaginable – with leather bands and colourful plastic beads (football fans buy them in the colours of their favourite club) at a very cheap price; with a yellow band and tassels; and ones with yellow plastic beads or the more sophisticated ones made of amber (the most traditional version). The best things come in small packages such as one with a metallic band and silver- or gold-plated beads. *Kombolóia* can also be bought in larger sizes for use as wall hangings.

Leather goods
Handbags, sandal, and such accessories as wallets or belts are considerably cheaper than, for example, in Western Europe – but the quality is often not as high. An insider's tip: shoes are

of a high quality and very reasonably priced.

Music
On Rhodes, you can buy any music that is internationally popular, on CDs, records or cassette tapes. For high quality, you pay about the same amount as you would at home. There is also a large selection of Greek music to choose from. A few names to look for: Mános Chatzidákis; Dioníssis Savvópoulos (an old rocker whose songs, such as *Those Bloody Greeks*, were shocking in their time); Eléni Karaíndrou (among others, the music for Theó Angelópolous's *The Beekeeper*); Vangélis Papathanassíou (known by his first name in foreign countries, and for film soundtracks such as the music to Costa Gravas's *Missing*); Jórgas Daláras (known especially for traditional Rembítiko songs, but also for pop and Latin American music); Cháris Alexíou (who interprets traditional and modern pieces - a number of young singers have copied her singing style); and Níkos Papázoglou (Rembítiko songs, pop music). As for the prolific works of Míkis Theodorákis, also a much talked-about politician, we can recommend María Farantoúri's intrepretation of his song cycles. Maybe you can find some music you like – it'll add to the authenticity of your Greek evening at home.

Furs
Fur coats and jackets are a hit with tourists on Rhodes. There are more than 100 fur shops on the island. Many of the furs sold on Rhodes come from Kastoriá in northern Greece. They specialize in small fur pieces there. The furriers cut the fur into thin strips and then sew them together into one large piece. The "pieced together" coats and jackets look exactly like furs that came from one hide, but are far less expensive. Remember, though, that with furs it's always advisable to haggle over the price.

Sponges
The famous sponge-diving island Kálymnos, which is one of the Dodecanese islands, supplies Rhodes with yellow and brown natural sponges. During the sponge season, divers can sometimes be seen calling at the Mandráki Harbour, selling the fruit of their risky labour directly.

Rugs, material, crochet work
In recent years, many women have taken the loom out of storage again and sell *kelims* (oriental wall hangings) and material, for example, to be used for bed throws. A "stronghold" of carpet weaving is Archángelos. Many weavers have no objections if someone looks over their shoulder while they're working. It's usually enough just to ask in a *kafeníon* for the address of a weaver. Before you start on your way, you should bear in mind that villages on Rhodes have their own daily routines. Coming to someone's house between 1 pm and 5 pm is considered rude, at least in summer, and hardly any woman is sitting at her loom in the afternoon heat. Delicate knitting and crochet work are frequently offered, however, they are not always "Made in Rhodes".

Donkey races at the parish fair

Thanks to the saints, almost every village has at least one joyful festival a year, which calls for music and dancing until the wee hours of the morning

PUBLIC HOLIDAYS

1 January *New Year's Day*
The name day of all those named Vassílis (masculine) or Vassilikí (feminine) was formerly a more important celebration than Christmas. In Greece, Saint Vassílios brings presents to the children. On New Year's Eve, the men play cards in order to test their luck, and often lose considerable amounts of money in the process. On New Year's morning, children go door-to-door singing and are given a sweet or a little money in return. When families cut the "New Year's cake", they believe that whoever finds the lucky coin has a lucky year ahead.

6 January *Epiphany*
On Epiphany, "the water is blessed". From the shore or a ship, the priest casts into the water a cross attached to a line and young men dive for it. The first man to reach it brings it back to the priest. The impressive ceremony takes place at the Mandráki Harbour on Rhodes.

Shrove Monday
26 February 2001; 18 March 2002; 10 March 2003

25 March *National Independence Day*
The 25th of March in 1821 marked the beginning of the Greek struggle for independence from the Turks. It is celebrated with parades in which school children must take part, often wearing national costumes or (younger ones) the blue, white-collared school uniform. On the same day, the church celebrates the Annuciation (on Rhodes in the Church on Mandráki Harbour). All men named Evángelos (Vangélis) and all women named Evanglía (Vangélio) have a name day that in Greece is more important than their own birthday.

Easter Sunday
15 April 2001; 5 May 2002; 27 April 2003
For Orthodox Christians like the Greeks, Easter is the most important religious festival. Easter does not always fall on the same date

Rhodes wouldn't be Rhodes without its festivals. People feasting in traditional customs

MARCO POLO SELECTION: FESTIVALS

1 Parish Fair at Mesanagrós
On the Sunday after Easter, people from far and near stream to the Chapel of St Thomas (page 35)

2 Pilgrimage to the Tsambíka Monastery
Here, the traditional piety still lives on (page 35)

3 Donkey Races in honour of Saint Soulás
A festival held near Soroní in honour of the Apostle Paul's companion (page 35)

4 Mammut-Panijíri in Kremastí
The largest parish fair of the Dodecanese islands is celebrated for nine days (page 35)

for Catholics and Protestants. Strict Orthodox Christians fast for 49 days before Easter. The fasting period, Lent, begins on Shrove Tuesday, which many people celebrate with a picnic. The highlights of the Easter festival are the procession on Good Friday and the midnight mass, which begins late Saturday night: The people hold unlit candles in their hands and it's almost completely dark in the church. At midnight, the priest says "Look and you shall receive the light" and lights a candle. The candle's flame is passed from candle to candle until the entire church is brightly lit by candlelight. Bringing home the Easter candle with its burnt wick is considered to be a good omen. After the Easter "fireworks", the gourmet feast begins: soup made from innards is served that same night, and, in the morning, lamb is turned on spits everywhere. Until Easter Monday (and often until Tuesday), there's eating, drinking and dancing – even the smallest villages are full of life. As many relatives as possible travel from Athens or even from foreign countries to return to their villages for the celebrations. Easter eggs in Greece are red, a symbol for the blood of Christ.

1 May *Labour Day*

21 May *Festival of Emperor Constantine and Empress Helena (Eléni)*
Name day of all people who are named after these saints (an estimated one-third of the population, including many public figures and quite a few politicians). In earlier times, schools were even closed on this day.

15 August *Dormition of the Virgin, Assumption Day*
The most important religious holiday, next to Easter, especially observed in the Churches dedicated to the Virgin Mary (for example, in Kremastí, Émbonas).

28 October *National Holiday*
"No Day" as a remembrance of how the Greek general Ioánnis Metaxás responded to the ultimatum given by Italy, the then wartime enemy. Celebrated much like 25 March, but with less ado.

24–26 December *Christmas*
A less important holiday in the past, but in recent years, especially in the cities, it's become more commercialized and more about feasting than about religion.

LOCAL FESTIVALS

Panijíri (parish fair) is held at least once a year in every village, always on the name day of the patron saint to whom the church is dedicated. There is almost always a church service held on the eve before the fair, and the celebration is held afterwards on the church or village green – with plenty of music, dancing and good food. On Patronage Day itself, another church service is held in the morning, and another celebration can't be ruled out.

March
Shrove Monday: *Carnival procession* in Kremastí

April
23 April: *Name day of St George,* celebrated, for example, in Afántou and Kritinía. If Easter is after this date, the festival falls on Easter Monday

Traditional folk dancing

Sunday after Easter: *St Thomas* ★ Festival of the Chapel of the Saint in Mesanagrós

May
First week of May: *Flower Festival* with a procession of floats, Mandráki, city of Rhodes
21 May: *St Constatine,* Thári

June
24 June: *Solstice*
29 June: Festival in honour of Saints *Peter and Paul,* Líndos

July
12 July: *Archangel Gabriel,* Kámiros Monastery
17 July: *Prophet Elias,* on Mt Profítis-Ilías (the chapel is located next to the hotel)
27 July: *St Panteleímon,* Siánna
30 July: *St Soulás,* ★ Soroní

August
6 August: Transfiguration of Christ, near Maritsá (near Psínthos in the Koumboúli mountains)
14–23 August: *Virgin Mary,* ★ Kremastí

September
8 September: *Birth of the Virgin Mary.* Celebrations ★ in lower Tsambíka Monastery and in Skiádi Monastery
14 September: *Tímios Stavrós.* The traditional "Holy Cross" in Kalithiés, Malónas and Apóllonas

October
18 October: *Luke the Evangelist,* Afántou

November
8 November: *Taxiarchen.* Archángelos honours its patron saints, the archangels

Fortified walls under blue skies

There's always something to see and do in this medieval city

A swim in the ocean in the morning, followed by a walk along the city wall affording views of Turkish mosques and a stroll through the shops of the old town in the afternoon. Round out the day with a visit to the ancient temple in the city, then treat yourself to dinner in a top-class restaurant on the water. Finally, after midnight has come and gone, you can sit back and listen to *bousoúki* music in a pub. This is how a day in Rhodes can be. A trip through the millenniums, from ancient Greece to the present day, filled with such an abundance of diverse and often conflicting impressions that you hardly have time to digest them all.

As hectic as any modern city in the world; as sleepy as a little old village in Provence; impressive walls from the age of chivalry are juxtaposed with tasteless, hastily built buildings; minarets and ornate, unpretentious marble columns of ancient temples – all these contrasts make up the city of Rhodes.

The sky over the roofs of Rhodes city is an enticing blue

Hotel and restaurant prices

Hotels
Category 1: above 33,800 Dr
Category 2: 22,550-33,800 Dr
Category 3: below 22,550 Dr

Prices are for two persons staying in a double room, including breakfast

Restaurants
Category 1: more than 7,350 Dr
Category 2: 4,500-7,350 Dr
Category 3: below 4,500 Dr

Prices include a starter, a main course, dessert, and wine

It's a place that virtually provokes controversy. Some say that it's best to just ignore the island capital of Rhodes when making an island sight-seeing tour. The quickly thrown together houses, extremely ugly hotels, fast-food joints, tacky souvenirs en masse, traffic and crowded beaches are not recommended. Others swear by the beauty and charm of the Old Town, the fascination of the port and the impressive selection of shops and boutiques. Where else can you find traces of three centuries and (at least) three cultures, from a wealthy ancient Greek woman's filigree bangle bracelet to a completely preserved medieval shopping street, and all in such a small space? Where else are holidaymakers offered such a variety of entertainment, good restaurants, pubs and amazing dances that you are welcome to join in on.

As is always the case, the truth lies somewhere in the middle. Everything that both fans and critics say about the city of Rhodes is true. But if you give the city the cold shoulder and immediately keep on driving to a small holiday apartment on the east coast, you'll miss out on an exciting adventure that's rich in contrasts.

Like a giant octopus, the city reaches its tentacles out to all sides, overgrowing the suburbs and twining itself around nearby villages – it's so crowded, that sometimes you can tell where the border is only by the looking at the town sign. A typical recurring question that arriving tourists ask the tour bus operator who has picked them up from the airport and driven along the west coast towards the island's capital: "Are we in the city of Rhodes yet?" They ask it for the first time in Paradíssi, the second time in Ialyssós and the third time in Ixiá. The hotel they have book-

MARCO POLO SELECTION: CITY OF RHODES

1 Old Town
Every stone is worth seeing – even if too many tourists already know this. Take a walk through the narrow streets, perhaps you can take a look at one of the courtyards (page 40)

2 Rodíni Park
Recover from the bustle of the city with a picnic out in the open (page 54)

3 Folk Dance Theatre
At Nélli Dimóglou's theatre, you can experience authentic Greek dances – learn them for yourself in a crash course (page 51)

4 Filérimos
Ancient ruins, a romantic monastery, a herbal liqueur and Rhodes from a bird's eye view – an oasis on the outskirts of town (page 52)

ed is probably there, but the inner city is still some 10 km away. Twenty years ago, Ixiá was an insignificant town on the west coast. Today, it's part of the city of Rhodes (although unofficial).

The hotels are located one after the other along the whole stretch of the coast. Most of them are tall, bulky and painted grey or perhaps white. Here again is evidence of the rampant development of the 1960s and 1970s that spoiled so many southern European coasts. It's too bad that the tour bus doesn't continue driving straight around the cape. If you're walking round the cape, behind a bend, out of the blue, you'll see what looks like a small, light-coloured building literally surrounded by hotels and cafeterias, located on a promontory pointing curiously into the ocean. For many newcomers, the Rhodes Aquarium is the first sign of the BT era – Before Tourism.

The three districts of the city are arranged around the harbour basin like pieces of a very large and simple puzzle. In the centre, at the commercial port, lies the Old Town. It belongs to the locals in the winter and the tourists in the summer. The second district, close to Mandráki Harbour, is full of hotels, souvenir shops and fast-food restaurants. In summer, it's full of life; in winter, the district's closed doors and shutters are very uninviting to tourists who come here out of season.

The biggest piece of the puzzle is the residential area of Rhodes city. The houses and streets could be in any city in southern Europe. Here people live, get up and go to work in the morning, and return home in the evening. Most of the shops sell articles of everyday life: jeans and sweatshirts, school books and chewing gum, sauce pans and vases. There is hardly anything there that reminds you of a holiday resort.

In the evenings people make their way to Mandráki Harbour, the Old Town or to one of the surrounding villages. The speciality restaurants and dance halls couldn't exist without the regulars from Rhodes city.

The residential area is separated from the Old Town by the old city walls and green spaces. It's widest at the south-east, becomes more narrow and nestles into the houses of the Old Town like a soft shawl.

Exploring the city of Rhodes by car is nerve-racking for non-locals. While the local driver confidently manoeuvres his or her car through the small, tightly packed streets and actually reaches his or her destination, the tourist, with map in hand, is at a complete loss as to what to do and instead ends up in front of a round, red sign with a white bar ("Residents Only!"). Almost everyone starts thinking that there's a one-way street for each of the 43,500 residents of Rhodes city.

Bicyclists who take traffic rules literally may find themselves passing by the aquarium two or three times before they finally find a opening. A special difficulty for non-locals is the habit of the officials of frequently changing the direction of one-way streets. You're driving down a street, always following the

direction of the blue, arrow-shaped sign when you suddenly see a white arrow pointing in the direction you just came from. Don't panic, the one-way street was indeed going in the other direction yesterday (or four weeks or a year ago)!

It's easiest just to take the bus, for example at 28 Odós Oktovríou. You can take line 1, 2 or 4 to Mandráki Harbour or directly to the old city wall at the commercial port (Emborikó limáni). Or you can walk along the water. Walking is highly recommended in the Old Town as well.

★ The Old Town in Rhodes city is tricky. It fascinates, confuses, drives you astray. You begin your exploration slowly, marvelling at the Knights Road that looks as though the people who lived there 500 years ago have simply vanished into their houses. You continue on, past the Palace of the Grand Masters, stroll a little down Odós Sokrátous, the shopping street and stop for something to drink in the Café Kárpathos …

Whenever it suits you, you turn off to a path, fascinated by an entrance overgrown with countless flowers. You follow the narrow lane that twists and turns to the right, to the left and to the right again … You pass by the Turkish baths, the folk dancing theatre, eat a little tasty snack, buy a couple of sweet treats in a tiny bakery – soon your feet are ready for a break …

You can spend entire days in the Old Town and always discover something new. There are more than 30 buildings and sites worth seeing. For many cities, just one of these sights would be enough to merit a trip to the historical heart. The Old Town of Rhodes is in essence a huge open-air museum, but it is certainly not a stiff and dead one. Buildings are still partially used, for example, the archaeological authorities and other offices of the Greek Ministry of Culture are located on the street of the Knights. There are not many people who can say that they work in an office building from the middle ages! It's not unusual in the city of Rhodes.

The Old Town is not a place whose beauty is enjoyed only when it is devoid of people. Buildings come alive because of the people who live inside them as well as the tourists strolling by in amazement. During the high season, however, there just might be too many admirers. If you're there at this time, take a walk there in the early morning when the Old Town and its inhabitants are not so besieged by tourists.

☛ **City Map inside back cover**

SIGHTS

Please note: opening times and admission fees are subject to change. Fortunately, most of the buildings are close to one another and it can be pleasant to pass waiting periods by having a cup of coffee or rummaging through shops on Sokrátous street (where you might even forget your museum visit!).

Aquarium (U/B1)

Family outings on Rhodes can include both Rodíni Park and the aquarium, a heritage of the

Italian occupiers. In the graceful pavilion, you'd expect to see an Art Nouveau café rather than a hydro-biological institute. There's a biological museum in the basement and aquariums in which you can see fish and a variety of other sea life from the Greek waters: for example, bream, perch, spiny scorpion fish, sea urchins and starfish. *Daily 9.30 am–9 pm; admission 800 Dr; Kalímnou Lérou.*

Palace of the Grand Masters (U/C4)
The majestic castle is perched atop a hill overlooking the Old Town like a defiant landmark of the city. The Palace of the Grand Masters was once the centre of power of the Knights of St John of Jerusalem; it was the outpost of the Occident for 200 years in the fight against the Ottoman. Founded in Jerusalem by Italian traders, and formally recognized by the pope in 1099, the Order played an important role during the Crusades. Exiled from the Holy land, the Knights first arrived in Cyprus in 1291. In 1309, under the leadership of the Grand Master Foulquet de Villaret, they conquered Rhodes and made it into the largest fortified city in the Mediterranean region. After the Turkish conquered the island, the Order settled in Malta, which had been left to them by Emperor Charles V in 1530. The Knights of Malta originated from the Order of the Knights of St John of Jerusalem. The Grand Master reigned over the secular possessions like a ruler of a sovereign country. He was elected for life by select men from different sections of the Order ("tongues").

The Palace of the Grand Masters

The Palace as it looks today dates from the 1930s. The original edifice was built in the late 14th century. The main church is part of it. It was consecrated to Saint John of the Order and is located west of the entry hall.

After the Turkish conquered Rhodes (1522), the palace was used as a prison, the palace church as a cowshed and the main church as a mosque. Leftover gunpowder from the siege remained in the vault. In 1856, lightening struck, causing an explosion that destroyed the Church of St John. The surrounding buildings, among them the Palace of the Grand Masters, were severely damaged. Similar disasters have occcurred several times in Greece. The Parthenon Temple on the Acropolis sustained a large part of its damage through the explosion of a gunpowder magazine.

Only a few sections of the original building survived, among them, the entrance portal with both its semicircular towers. The Italian architects who restored the Palace of the Grand Masters were accused by the experts of doing a poor job. The palace was to have served as a representative residence of the Italian king and dictator Benito Mussolini should they ever come to visit Rhodes – which they never did.The palacce was renovated according to the tastes of the time, not restored to its original condition. One of the worse *faux pas*: the floor was inlaid with ancient mosaics from the Island of Kos, something that the knights or even the Grand Master himself would never have had in their rooms. Using artifacts and illustrations, two new exhibitions in the Palace of the Grand Masters describe how the people of Antiquity and the Middle Ages lived and worked. *July and Aug Mon 12.30 pm–3 pm, Tues–Sat 8.30 am–7 pm, Sun 8.30 am–3 pm, rest of the year Tues–Sun 8.30 am–3 pm; admission 1,200 Dr; Platía Kleovoúlou*

The twin towers of the harbour gates, with their fortified battlements

Mandráki Harbour (U/C–D3)
A name you should keep in mind: Mandráki. You'll be hearing the name over and over again whenever you ask how to get somewhere. Where is the tourist information centre? In Mandráki. Where can I find the market? In Mandráki. Where's a good place to rent a boat? Guess where? Mandráki means "little sheepfold". No one exactly knows how the ancient naval port in Rhodes City got its name. One explanation is that it could have something to do with the way it's built, for Mandráki Harbour resembles a pair of pliers and encloses the ships like a pen around a herd of sheep. If you come by ship into the harbour entrance, you'll be greeted by stags and does, the heraldic animals of the island. The Colossus of Rhodes supposedly stood here in ancient times. Coming from the ocean, on your left you can see the round tower of the mighty Ágios Nikólaos fortress dating from the 15th century. The three mills on the pier are probably just as old. Mandráki is also the name of the area beyond the actual harbour. Buses and long-distance coaches depart regularly from Mandráki and a big taxi rank is located there as well. And then there's the market. The building of the Néa Agorá is not to be missed. It is heptagonal in shape, but is only one and a half storeys high. Many cafés are located under the arcade on the harbour side, which remain full late into the night. You can get the very popular (originally Turkish) sweets such as *baklavás* and *kataífi* here. International news-papers and magazines are sold at the two news-stands between the cafés. There's a fish market everyday except Sundays inside the Néa Agorá. There's also a couple of small restaurants and souvenir shops there. Unfortunately, the market has lost much of its original charm. Mandráki nevertheless continues to fascinate: the harbour atmosphere, the hurly-burly of the market, big-city bustle. Naturally, this jewel has many admirers. Some days, there are so many of them that they trip over each other at the Eleftherías (Freedom) gate, which leads to the most direct way to the Old Town. Cars also pass through the Eleftherías gate, and there is only a narrow pedestrian walkway on each side.

Monte Smith (U/A6)
Like every Greek city that has its orgins in ancient Greece, Rhodes city has its own acropolis. Unfortunately, there is not much left of the temples. A trip to the top of this roughly 110-m-high hill is still worthwhile, however, because you can see the entire city from the top. Old and new, beautiful and ugly, its seemingly ill-befitting name goes back to the commander-in-chief of the British Marine Corps that were stationed on Rhodes in the early 19th century. Their task was to monitor the eastern Mediterranean region and protect it from potential attacks by Napoleon's troops. At that time,

Napoleon was conducting his military campaign in Egypt.

The Italians named the mountain Monte Santo Stefano. It's still sometimes called by that name today. It's located in the west of the city and is easily reached by the public bus service. Three and a half pillars of a Temple of Apollo, a restored theatre and a partly reconstructed stadium are all that's left. However, it's enough to give you an impression of how it used to look.

From Monte Smith, you can admire the city of Rhodes in all its Mediterranean charm. "Scenic" view number one is found right away, where the tour buses are parked. From the rim of the hill, the west coast village of Ixía presents itself as a lump of rampant asphalt and concrete. Major hotels, such as the Sofitel Capsis, rise into the sky.

To enjoy scenic view number two (and this time we're not being sarcastic about the scenic part!), you have to climb to the highest peak of Monte Smith, where the foundations of two temples can be seen. From there, you have a view of the west coast towards Sími Island and Asia Minor, which lies beyond the airport. It's especially nice to enjoy this panorama during sunset. *You can always get there via Odós Voríou Ipírou in the New City, bus no. 5 from Mandráki/Néa Agorá*

Rejab Pascha Mosque (U/D5)

When the Turkish conquered Rhodes in 1522, they gave the city an entirely new look. Domed edifices with minarets, unknown to Rhodes up to then, were erected. Churches were turned into mosques, storage places or cowsheds. Some of the churches were abandoned. The buildings of the Turkish era met a similar fate when the Italians invaded; then they were either neglected or converted for different purposes. Some of the mosques are presently being restored, albeit very slowly, so that most of them can be admired only from the outside.

The same is true of the Rejab Pascha Mosque at the little Platía Doriéos in the centre of the Old Town. It's the most beautiful mosque on Rhodes, above all because of its once famous faience furnishings. At present, visitors can enjoy only the picturesque view of the minaret and fountain. *Platía Doriéos*

Knights Road (U/C–D4)

Straight as a die, the Odós Ippotón spans from the Order Hospital of the Knights of St John of Jerusalem (which today houses the archaeology museum) to the Palace of the Grand Masters. To the right and left are the former hostels of the various "tongues" of the Order, decorated with the coats of arms of each Grand Master. The nicest hostels, which belonged to the French knights, are located in the centre. Knights Road is the only medieval residential street to have been preserved on Rhodes. It's a very Spartan street and is quite dull when there aren't any people around. *May be visited any time, but viewing the interior areas is prohibited. Odós Ippotón, Old Town*

City walls (U/C–E4–6)

For the best views of the minaret and courtyards of the

Old Town, head for the city walls. You can get to the main wall by way of the Cannon Gate of the Palace of the Grand Masters Loggia. The Palace of the Grand Masters is located higher than the rest of the old town. The Cannon gate is open two days a week for a short time. If you can't make it during the opening times and still want to get an impression of the grand city walls and gates, you can start from Eleftherías gate and make your way around the city walls from the outside – the trip takes about one hour. *Palace of the Grand Masters; Mon and Sat 2.45 pm; admission 1,200 Dr*

Suleiman Mosque **(U/C5)**
The pink building on the upper end of Odós Sokrátous (the shopping street) dates from the 19th century and is a reconstruction of the mosque that was built immediately after the capture of Rhodes. *Usually closed to the public*

Turkish cemetery **(U/C2)**
An evocative place on the northern end of the Platía Eleftherías. The mosque at the centre is named after Murad Reis, an admiral who fell during the siege of Rhodes and is buried there. *May be visited any time, Platía Eleftherías, New Town*

Turkish baths **(U/C5)**
The large domed building from the 18th century today serves as a public bath (Dimotiká Lutrá), since many houses in the Old Town do not have their own bathtubs. Unfortunately, however, you won't find all the amenties of a genuine Turkish Hamam here, such as steam baths and massages. *Wed–Sat 7 am–7 pm; admission 500 Dr; Platía Aríonos, Old Town; Tel. 27 73 39*

Seaside road **(U/C2–3)**
The Eleftherías is so wide in some parts that cars seem to get swallowed up in it. Imposing, neoclassical-looking buildings line the right and left sides of the road. The post office, for example, is located in the stately building that once served as official offices of Turkish prefects and Italian governors.

Across from it, next to the Bishop's palace, is the Orthodox Evangelismós Church. This former main church of the St John of Jerusalem Knights was reconstructed from old drawings in 1925. *7 am–12 pm and 5.30 pm–7.30 pm*

Clock Tower **(U/C4–5)**
It's worth the effort to climb this tower, because at the top you are presented with wonderful views of the roofs and towers of the Old Town. The clock chimes right on time! *Daily 9 am–7 pm and 9 pm–11 pm; admission incl. soft drink 1,000 Dr; 1 Odós Orféos, Old Town*

MUSEUMS

Museum of Archaeology **(U/D4)**
The former Order Hospital of the Knights, the building which houses the museum, is especially worth seeing. It dates from the 15th century and is a simple building with a large courtyard that is surrounded on all sides by arcades. One side is entirely taken up by a 50-m-long former Ward of Knights. The hospital was supposed to be one of the best in its time,

so much so that patients from foreign countries even came to it.

The greatest treasures of the museum include a small marble statue dating from c. 100 BC called *Aphrodite Crouching*; a tomb from the fifth century that shows two women, probably mother and daughter (according to the inscription on the stone, their names were Krito and Timarista); and a large statue of Aphrodite that was found in the sea near Rhodes. *Tues–Sun 8.30 am–3 pm, July and Aug. Mon 12.30–7 pm, Tues–Fri 8 am–7 pm, Sat and Sun 8.30 am–3 pm; admission 800 Dr; Odós Apéllou, Old Town*

Icon Exhibition **(U/D4)**
The little church of the Virgin Mary (12th century) provides the right ambience for a collection of icons and murals. Sacral music played from a tape sets the right tone for visitors to the exhibition. In the cool room filled with images of saints on dark wood, everybody instinctively lowers their voices and notices that this is a place to recover from the impressions of the loud and turbulent city and just contemplate. *Tues–Sun 8.30 am–3 pm; admission 600 Dr; Panagía tou Kástrou (St Mary), Platía Mousseíon*

Museum of Decorative Arts **(U/D4)**
An ethnic museum with a large collection plates from Líndos. *Tues–Sun 8.30 am–3pm; admission 500 Dr; Platía Argirokástrou, Old Town*

Municipal Picture Gallery **(U/D4)**
With this institution, Rhodes is a step ahead of most other provincial Greek towns. With the exception of Athens, there are only a few opportunities to get an overview of contemporary art in Greece. In this small gallery, you'll find works by pioneers of 20th-century Greek painting, such as Fótis Kóntoglou and Spíros Vassilíou, as well as paintings and sculptures by contemporary artists. *Mon–Sat 8 am–2 pm; admission 500 Dr; Platía Símis, Old Town*

RESTAURANTS

Like all Greek city-dwellers, the inhabitants of Rhodes are passionate about eating, and are willing to drive a few kilometres for a good meal. The selection of good restaurants in both Rhodes city and the surrounding villages is so vast that you just can't try all of them.

Akropolis **(U/D5)**
Outdoor restaurant with many tasty specialities. *16 Odós Sofokléous, Old Town; Tel. 29745; category 2*

Casbah **(U/D5)**
Stylish café and restaurant serving Mediterranean and Middle Eastern cuisine. *4–8 Odós Platónos, Old Town; Tel. 73636; category 1*

Cleo's **(U/D5)**
Good Italian and French cooking. Open only in the evenings. *17 Odós Agíou Fanouríou, Old Town; Tel. 28415; category 1*

Diafani **(U/C5)**
This *tavérna*, which is situated on the same square as the Turkish baths, offers a large selection of cooked dishes. If

you order the Greek Plate, you will be served a colourful assortment of what the kitchen of this inexpensive restaurant offers. *3 Platía Ariónos, Old Town; Tel. 26053; category 3*

Dinóris **(U/D4)**
If you like fish, this place is for you. The restaurant specializes in seafood in all variations. An extra bonus (which, however, may be reflected a little in the prices): at Dinóris, you'll be eating in a beautiful historic building. *14 a Platía Mousío, Old Town; Tel. 25824; category 1*

Hollands **(U/A2)**
Dutch restaurant that serves very good Indonesian food in addition to the numerous types of pancakes that are a special favourite among children. *20 Aktí Miaoúli, New Town; category 2*

Líndos **(U/B1)**
A relatively modest restaurant that serves good Greek food. The proof is in the pudding: locals often come here to eat lunch. *Platía Gavriíl Charítas, New Town; Tel. 24421; category 2*

Mama Sofia **(U/C4)**
Tavérna with reasonably priced fish dishes and an informal atmosphere. *28 Odós Orféos; Tel. 24469; category 2*

Oasis **(U/D5)**
Serves exclusively Greek dishes, cooked in traditional ways. *Platía Doriéos, Old Town, category 2*

Pandaisia **(U/D5)**
This pleasant restaurant is owned by a friendly family from Ólimbos (on the neighbouring island of Kárpathos) who offer good, plain Greek cooking. As is the norm in their home village, the proprietor wears her traditional outfit – which is not done for tourists. Very good value for the money! *Platía Akousiláou, Old Town; category 3*

Socratous Garden **(U/C5)**
An outdoor restaurant in the Old Town where you can eat very good Greek food while sitting under palm trees. Wicker chairs and two long counters also welcome guests who just want an ice cream or something to drink. How about trying the speciality of the house: melon schnapps? *126 Odós Socratoús; Tel. 20153; category 3*

Symposium **(U/C5)**
If you like the Old Town atmosphere and Greek cuisine, be sure and come to this restaurant. It is located in a restored Old Town house. You'll find *mezédes* such as stuffed grape leaves and aubergine paste *(melitzanosaláta)*, as well as main dishes like braised beef or grilled scampi, on the menu. *Odós 3 Archélou, Old Town; Tel. 37509; category 2*

SHOPPING

Shopping is a constant temptation because of the numerous stores and there's so much to be had at good prices. For example, there is an abundance of good clothing stores that carry internationally known brands in the New Town.

Brouzakis **(U/C3)**
All you need for your holiday pictures! Here you can buy film,

batteries and other necessities for the (amateur) photographer on holiday. This dealer also offers quick picture developing that is popular all throughout Greece. Your photos can be developed and ready to be picked up in just one hour. *47 Odós Sofoklí Venizélo, New Town*

Casts & Reproductions **(U/D4)**
If you've seen a piece in the Museum of Archaeology that particularly caught your eye, go a few more steps and you might just be able to buy (or at least order) a replica of it at the shop run by the Greek Ministry of Culture. *Corner of Odós Apéllou/ Knights Road*

Ilías Laloúnis **(U/D4)**
In this branch of this internationally renowned Athenian jewellery designer (also in Paris, London, New York and Geneva), you'll feel like the sympathetic but destitute Holly, played by Audrey Hepburn in the classic film *Breakfast at Tiffany's*: everything sparkles so seductively, but you can't afford to buy anything.

After some hunting, you might discover something after all that isn't totally out of your price range. Don't dispair! *Platía Megalou Alexándrou, Old Town*

Manuel **(U/C3)**
This is a well-stocked record shop in the New Town. You can find Greek CDs, records and music cassettes of excellent quality (don't hesitate to ask for advice!), as well as anything that is currently popular internationally. *25 Odós, 11–13 Martíou*

Marco Polo Gallery **(U/D 5)**
Contemporary art, tastefully presented (however, not exactly inexpensive). *Odós Agíou Fanoúriou 42, Old Town*

Nikos & Takis **(U/C4)**
The Athenian Nobel designer offers up his collection for sale on three floors of a former Turkish harem. Among his collection are sheer blouses, hand-painted scarves and elegant clothing, but beware: the beautiful wares run high in price. *26–28 Odós Panetíou*

HOTELS

Package tours usually have hotels outside the New Town of Rhodes. For a more quiet and atmospheric stay, choose one of the places within the Old Town walls. There is a vast selection of small hotels and guest houses in all price categories that offer modern comfort combined with historical ambience.

Andreas Rooms **(U/D5)**
This small guest house is run by a Greek-French family who also speak fluent English. There are rooms available with and without a shower/WC. Room number 21, with its three windows, is by far the nicest. You can sit and admire the view from the bar on the terrace that overlooks the entire Old Town. *12 rooms; 28 d Odós Omírou; Tel. 34156; Fax 74285; category 3*

Casa de la Sera **(U/E5)**
Centrally located, this old house from the times of the Order of the Knight is run by the Delasera

Miracles happen

The often-admired and sometimes cursed Greek calm composure does not just have its roots in the sunny climate, but also in the natural faith of the Hellenes. They know that they can always turn to the responsible saint if they have a problem. The saint does not only linger in the heavenly realm, but is, for the most part, somebody nearby to turn to: in the form of an icon in a church, in one's living room, on the bridge of a ferry or on the windscreen of a public service bus.

St Paraskeví is responsible for eye problems, St Markélla takes care of the legs, St Nikólaos sees to children and sailors, St Raffaíl cures supposedly incurable diseases and illnesses – and the Mother of Christ, elsewhere called the Virgin Mary, can help out in all cases.

family. It is located in the Old Town, only 200 m away from the ferry dock. There's a bar on the ground floor and a roof terrace as well. *8 rooms; 38 Odós Thiséos; Tel. 75154; no fax; category 2*

Irini **(103/E–F2)**
Located immediately next to the Chapel of St Irene in Koskinoú, this small block of apartments is run by a married couple by the name of Rados. It is well-suited for holidaymakers who want to stay in a quiet, rather authentic "Greek" village. To Maris Rados, guests are a part of the family, and if she cannot express herself in a given language, her eldest daughter helps her out. The village itself has several good *tavérnas* and restaurants, *kafénias* and shops, as well as a supermarket. Since the bus connection is bad, we recommend that you arrange to have your own vehicle. *Koskinoú, 8 km from Rhodes city; 10 rooms; Tel. 63000 and 61944; no fax; category 2*

Marco Polo Mansion **(U/D5)**
Five lavishly furnished rooms in a former Turkish house, with harem and hamam. *42 Odós Agíou Fanoúriou, Old Town; Tel./Fax 79115; e-mail: marcopologallery@hotmail.com; category 1*

Niki's Rooms **(U/D5)**
The stylishly furnished guest house is pretty centrally located. *12 rooms; 39 Odós Sofokléou, Old Town; Tel. 25115; no fax; category 3*

Olympos **(U/D5)**
Guest house open all-year round, in an old house with a nice garden. *7 rooms, 56 Odós Fanoúriou, Old Town; Tel./Fax 33567; category 3*

Rodos Park **(U/B4)**
Comfortable, close to the Old Town, has a pool. Located approximately. 800 m from the beach. All rooms have double divans; suites with whirlpools. Open all-year long. *60 rooms; 12 Odós Ríga Feréou; Tel. 24612; Fax 24613; category 1*

S. Nikolis' Hotel (U/C5)

Sotiris Nikolis and his wife, Marianne, a Danish woman, have turned several old town houses from the 14th century into a small hotel with 12 rooms, five apartments, and four honeymoon suites, each with their own garden and balcony, as well as private parking spaces. The rooms are tastefully furnished in traditional style. All have telephones and baths. Up to now, Americans have been the most frequent guests here. For an extra charge, there's a breakfast buffet on a large terrace with a nice view. *61 Odós Ippodámou; Tel. 3456; Fax 32034; category 1*

SPORTS & LEISURE

Mopeds and motorcycles

There are many rental places in the New Town. One specializes in Harley Davidson motorcycles: *Harley, 28 Odós, 80 Oktovríou; Tel./Fax 74925*

Bicycling

Rhodes is a mountainous island. If you want to rent a bicycle, you should rent a mountain bike. Top-class mountain bikes can be rented at *Hellas Bike Travel* in *Grecotel Rhodos Imperial* in Ixiá *(Tel. 7250920; Fax 7257671).* English-speaking tours of the island (at varying levels of difficulty) are also offered there.

Horse-Riding

In Greece, horses are still predominantly used for farm work. One of the two riding stables on Rhodes is located on the way to Mount Filérimos. *Mike's Horses, Odós Keramedénia; daily 9.30 am–1.30 pm, 4 pm–8 pm; Tel. 21387*

Water sports

Water sports enthusiasts are not left wanting in Rhodes city and its environs. You can rent surfboards and pedal boats, or give water-skiing a try, on any of the large beaches. The best wind for surfing is on the west coast.

Boats of conventional sizes all the way up to sailboats suitable for competition can be rented (with or without crew) in Mandráki Harbour. For information contact: *Yacht Agency Rhodos, 1 Odós Virónos, New Town; Tel. 22927; Fax 23393; www.yachtagency.com*

ENTERTAINMENT

You won't find as wide a selection of entertainment anywhere on the island as you will in the city of Rhodes. Bear in mind that pubs where live music is played either don't open until 11 pm or are totally empty until then.

Café Chantant (U/D5)

This is not a café, but rather a typically Greek music pub where from around ten o'clock musicians and singers play Greek music almost continuously. When Greeks are in full swing, they dance. Foreigners, however, should restrict themselves to just watching. A drink costs about £ 5; Greeks prefer to have an entire bottle of whiskey served at the table (about £ 50). *Tues–Sun 11.30 pm–3 am; 22 Odós Aristotélous, Old Town; Tel. 32277*

Harley Davidson Bar (U/C3)

A trendy club that's not just for the motorcycle fans who enjoy drinking cocktails and long

The beaches on Rhodes offer more than just swimming

drinks on real Harley saddles. *25 Odós Martiou/Odós Amerikís, New Town*

Casino **(U/B2)**
In 1999, the time-honoured building of the former *Hotel des Roses,* which dates from the Italian occupation, was converted into an elegant casino, directly on the ocean. Roulette wheels spin 365 days a year in the same place where the heads of government of EU countries met in 1988. Hugh Hefner, founder of the Playboy empire, owns part of the casino, so don't be surprised if you are served by white bunnies. *Odós Ko; minimum age: 23; admission 5,000 Dr*

Elli **(U/C2)**
Guests in this club are entertained with Rembétiko songs until the first person gets up to dance. A typical lyric: "Take your dirty, unwashed, thrown-out things and get lost, my friend. What do you still want from me?" *6 Aktí Kountouriót, New Town; Tel. 26800*

Le Palais **(U/C3)**
Disco - big, loud and colourful. *25 Martío, New Town*

Light shows **(U/C4)**
Ignore all your reservations about such a spectacle, this one is worth it. The focus is the Palace of the Grand Masters, whose history comes alive through catchy texts and skilful light and smoke effects. *April–Oct daily shows in several languages (see sign next to ticket box office); admission 1,500 Dr; Platía Rimíni; Tel. 21922*

Nélli Dimóglou Folk Dance Theatre **(U/C5)**
★ The idea comes from Athens. The renowned dance instructor Dóra Strátou founded her own dance theatre in Athens ten years ago. One of her pupils, Nélli Dimóglou, copied her

idea. The ensemble performs traditional Greek folk dances, in the costumes of each region. After seeing the performance, you leave with an impression of how Greek dances are "correctly" danced. Classic folk songs are also performed. For groups of five or more who want to learn the steps themselves, Nélli Dimóglou regularly conducts one-week-long crash courses. *Price per person and course, with free admission to the theatre, approx. 50,000 Dr, to register, ring 20157.*

Daily performances during the season, except Sat, at 9.20 pm, Mon, Wed, Fri also 11.30 pm; Odós Andronikou 7, Old Town; admission for all seats 3,000 Dr; Tel. 29085

INFORMATION

Greek Tourism Office **(U/C3)**
Mon–Fri 7.30 am–3 pm; corner of Makaríou and Papágou streets; Tel. 23255; Fax 26955

City of Rhodes Tourist Association **(U/C4)**
Platía Rimini, Mandráki; Mon–Sat 9 am–8 pm; Tel. 35945

SURROUNDING AREA

The surrounding area – which actually covers the entire island. We'll remain in the vicinity of the city first, then move on to recommend excursions further afield. The harbour is the ideal starting point for island-hopping – for example, you can be on Kos or Kárpathos in just about four hours – or for a day trip to the Turkish coast.

Filérimos **(103/D-E2)**
★ To a resident of the city of Rhodes, Mount Filérimos is a very popular local recreation area. It is relatively cool even in summer on the 267-m-high plateau and the path to the top provides a stunning view of the coast. The acropolis of ancient Ialyssós once stood here.

You can begin by leaving the city via the west coast street and turn left at Triánta. The path is marked by signs. Make sure you have plenty of time for the trip up the mountain; the winding roads do not allow you to drive at high speeds. After only 20 minutes away from the hurly-burly of the inner city, you are in a completely different world: stately pine trees to your right and left, the aroma of herbs, chirping cicadas. You can hear from far away if someone with a car or a moped is approaching. Translated, Filérimos means "friend of loneliness". Allegedly, the mountain was given its name in medieval times, when a hermit settled region there.

The buildings and ruins on Mt. Filérimos date back three millenniums. The monastery dating from the tenth century is the best preserved. Italian archaeologists reconstructed it on the ruins of the old buildings before World War II. The monastery church, also reconstructed by the Italians, was built by Crusaders in the 15th century, and, today is used as a site for romantic weddings as well as baptisms.

At first glance, it's hard to see the Chapel of Ágios Geórgios

Chostós. It's set a good way into the slope as the name Chostós (buried, hidden) suggests. The frescoes inside illustrate scenes from the life of Christ (among them, the Betrayal of Judas, the Flagellation and the Crucifixion), as well as kneeling knights and the eight-point cross of the Knights of St John of Jerusalem. Bear in mind, however, that the chapel is not open all the time.

At the top of the plateau, immediately in front of the monastery, are the rest of the small Athenian temples from the third and second century BC, an early Christian basilica, together with its preserved baptistry, and several chapels from the 15th and 16th centuries.

Continuing the tour, you can see the rest of the walls that were erected in the Byzantine era to protect the area from attacks. Mt. Filérimos was an important strategic point for the Knights of the St John, the Turks and the Italians. For this reason, the walls have been regularly maintained and repaired. Above all, the walk is rewarded with the views of the coast and the mountainous region in the south-west. At the kiosk by the ticket office, you can buy soft drinks and a liqueur called "Sette Erbe", named after the seven herbs it contains. *Excavation site open Tues–Fri 8.30 am–6 pm, Sat–Mon 8.30 am–3 pm; admission 800 Dr; the other paths may be used free of charge; 5 km from Ialyssós, bus from Rhodes City*

Kallithéa Thermal Springs (103/F3)
Before World War II, Rhodes had – apart from sun, sea and culture – another attraction on offer: a thermal bath. At the distinguished spa in Kallithéa on the east coast, affluent VIPs used to cure their rheumatism and other illnesses one didn't talk about, such as kidney disease or chronic constipation. Although the thermal bath was bombed during the war, most of the buildings were preserved, at least in part. Now an organization sees to their renovation. The buildings by Italian architect Pietro Lombardi have a Middle Eastern feel: the sulphureous spring, which, unfortunately, is dry these days, is surrounded by a dome-shaped building. Warm sunlight comes in through the windows and arcades. Palm trees add an exotic atmosphere. What the thermal bath might have looked like in its heyday can be seen in the episode *Holiday in Rhodes* of the English crime

The rocky bay of Kallithéa

series *The Adventures of Hercule Poirot.* Much of that drama – a story of jealousy that ends fatally – was filmed in 1989 in the Kallithéa thermal springs. It is presently being renovated and will soon be back in operation.

Kremastí **(103/D2)**
The attraction of this village on the west coast is the large church consecrated to the Panagía Kremastí (Hanging Mother of Christ) that is located at the entrance to the village (if you come from Rhodes city). Its second name, which is also the name of the village, can be traced back to a legend. As the story goes, an icon of the Virgin Mary was found hanging from an olive tree. A church for the Virgin Mary was then built on that exact spot. The icon is definitely worth seeing.

Kremastí (pop. 3,700) is the only place on Rhodes where a carnival procession is held on Shrove Monday. Jesters in colourful costumes, most of them children, parade through the village. Even more famous is the festival of the Virgin Mary, held from 14 to 23 August. During this time, not only are many masses conducted, but a large arts-and-crafts exhibition takes place as well. The Kremastí parish fair is the biggest spectacle of its kind on the Dodecanese Islands.

Rodíni Park **(103/E2)**
★ The greenbelt of Rhodes is located between Monte Smith and the road to Líndos. A small stream with waterfalls and ponds flows between pines, plane trees and cypresses. Stags and does, the heraldic animals of Rhodes, and Cretan wild goats are kept in a pen, and peacocks walk along the paths. Rodíni Park is at its prettiest in spring, of course. On Shrove Monday, many families come here for the traditional picnic that marks the beginning of the fasting period. Above the area, on a plateau, you can see several graves that were built into the rock. Travellers to Greece in the 19th century called the nicest grave the "Ptolemic Grave". The locals also call it *koúfio vounó*, hollow mountain. *Can be reached via the Odós Stéfanou Kasoúli or with bus no. 3 from Mandráki*

Sími **(109/D2)**
When everywhere in Greece picturesque old houses were being torn down and replaced by monotonous blocks of concrete in the name of "progress", the 2,500 residents of Sími Island restored their old houses or built new ones that strongly resembled the old ones. Today, they are reaping the benefits of this brillant decision: Sími is one of the most picturesque islands in the Aegean Sea. Especially popular are day excursions to the islet, which emerges in pastels from the sea after a two-hour-long boat ride. During the peak season, one boat after another docks between 11 am and 3 pm. Sími attractions include the large Panormítis Monastery,

The old houses have been lovingly restored on Sími Island

the upper area of the main village, from which there is a wonderful view overlooking the harbour, and the little beach called Pédi. If you decide to spend the night in Sími on the spur of the moment, be sure to inform your boat's captain and then inquire about a room in one of the hotels or tourist agencies at the harbour. In the evening, when the day tourists have gone, the island becomes even more idyllic and a hike around its interior is recommended. *Boats depart from Mandráki Harbour daily, no reservations taken; all tourist agencies can arrange excursions; another option is to take one of the ferries that depart several times a day*

Soroní **(102/C3)**
The "red" village on the west coast – more than one-third of the residents are said to vote for communist parties – is famous for its Pilgrimage Church of St Soulás, which is located about 4 km from Soroní on the road to Eleoússa. The name day of the patron saint is celebrated on 30 July, and a lively festival with plenty of food, dancing and a donkey race is held the day before. In any case the small village is worth visiting any time of the year because of the lovely woods surrounding it.

Tílos **(108/B-C2-3)**
This very tiny island (pop. 300) has only a small number of extremely loyal admirers who simply "let the wind flow through their hair" here. If you need all the bustle of city life, you should avoid Tílos! There are very few bars, and only one modest disco. Instead, it has beautiful, empty beaches. The main sights are the medieval Ágios Panteleímonas Monastery, the Crusaders' fortress of Megálo Chorió and the abandoned ghost town of Mikró Chorió, which comes to life only between 12 am and 5 am, when the music bar opens under the night sky. Accommodation can be arranged at the kiosk on the harbour.

Magical, mythical scenery

A huge open-air museum of Mediterranean culture, swimming on the east coast and peaceful villages in the hinterland

A medieval fortress perched atop a rocky outcrop, below, many snow-white houses nestled into the mountain. You can't find concrete or cars in this village. A picture from another era – that is why this tiny village (pop. 950), which the Greek government placed on the preservation list of historic buildings and monuments many years ago, is a major attraction – and this not only on Rhodes but in the entire country of Greece. Some people might find that fact unfortunate and think that placing a big "closed due to overcrowding" sign at the village entrance might soon be necessary. For half a year, from April to October, people push past the historic houses like in a department store during an end-of-season sale.

If you drive to Líndos by car or moped from Rhodes city, continue driving straight at the fork in the road after Kálathos, go past the hotels along the Vlícha bay and past the rock cliffs. You'll get the first and also the prettiest view of Líndos after a bend on the last leg of the road. It's worthwhile to stop, get out of the car and to enjoy the view that overlooks the fortress, houses and the beautiful beach. Usually, however, a few cars or a tour bus have already stopped there and a group of people can be seen taking pictures. Líndos has not been an insider tip for a long time now.

During high season, you'll have to come as early in the morning as possible to have the chance to find a nearby parking place and to be able to have an uninterrupted view of the houses. Between 9 and 10 am, the first tour busses begin to unload their human cargo on the Platía Eleftherías (Freedom Plaza). Taxis and municipal busses have their terminals here as well. Afterwards, you can

The columns of the Líndos acropolis attest to the town's past splendour

MARCO POLO SELECTION: LÍNDOS

1 Líndos acropolis
This fascinating historical site affords splendid ocean views (page 58)

2 Asklipión
An idyllic village with castle ruins and churches decorated with frescoes (page 64)

only walk or ride on the back of a mule to get around. So be prepared! The rattling, three-wheeled carts that carry the heavy luggage of guests in the holiday resorts are the only "motor vehicles" permitted on the narrow paths of Líndos, which are paved with round pebbles.

Odós Akropóleos leads to the centre of Líndos, but it is curiously much too narrow to use the term "street" for it. Travel agencies, cafés and souvenir shops skirt the few steps of the road until it reaches the donkey and mule parking place on the right side. For about 800 Dr, which you give to the owner before the ride begins, the patient animals transport tourists up the 116-m-high mountain, where the fortress is located.

Even though there are crowds pushing and pulling their way through, you should really stroll through the winding lanes at least once. The "captain houses" alone are worth seeing; they were built by wealthy local seafaring families during the Turkish occupation. You'll immediately notice the grey hewn stone that is found in very large quantities around Lárdos village; that's what gave the village its name.

You certainly don't have to miss out on swimming here in the seaport of Líndos. There is a bay with two very nice sandy beaches below the town (excursion boats from the city of Rhodes dock here as well), and at the back of the mountain is an almost closed bay called Ágios Pávlos. It is here that the Apostle Paul supposedly went ashore to convert the inhabitants of Líndos to Christianity. The entire village, including the white columns of the acropolis, is unfortunately best seen from the rubbish dump. (**107/F 2–3**)

SIGHTS

Acropolis

★ The mountain and fortress of Líndos offer a cross section of the history of the island within a narrow space. Evidence of all the important periods can be found here – ranging from flint tools from the Neolithic Period to the fortresses of the Crusaders that are so massive that everything else disappears behind them. The ancient structures were first exposed to daylight again by Danish archaeologists in the early 20th century. If you are walking, simply follow the signs. After you've gone about one-third of the way, you will pass the Church of the Virgin Mary. If you go by mule, you'll take a different, somewhat longer path to get there.

The mountain rises gradually from north to south, and has four plateaus. When you reach the first one, you can take a breather and enjoy the view of the beach. Here, you can see the entrances to three cisterns, a Byzantine tower and several column bases with inscriptions. They are part of the statues that wealthy citizens once donated for the holy shrine of Lindia the Athenian. What became of this statue can most likely be explained by the fact that, in the year 42, the Roman admiral and statesman Cassius Longinus (later he was involved in the murder of Caesar) arranged to have 3,000 statues moved from Rhodes to Rome, most of which came from Líndos.

The relief of a ship has been incised into the rock, a respect paid by the residents of Líndos to a successful general of the city who lived there in the year 2 BC.

The most strenuous part of the path is the "ascent" to the Knights of St John fortress. Some tired hikers might long for the end of the stony staircase, especially in summer. When you finally reach the top and pass through the arched entrance gate, you feel like you've suddenly stepped into antiquity: ancient altars on the walls and pedestals of monuments, outside is a wall and a couple of columns on top of it – ruins of a Hellenistic portico that span the entire length of the acropolis, 87 m.

The slender Doric columns of the Athena Temple, easily the most photographed subject of the site, are located all the way at the top of the fourth plateau. The part that is still preserved dates from the fourth century BC. At 22 m long and 8 m wide, the temple is relatively small. However, ancient structures that are so harmonic with their natural surroundings are rarely found in Greece. There are uninterrupted views in all directions, and one view appears more beautiful than all the others: the Ágios Pávlos bay in the south, with its small chapel. In the north, on the cape of the harbour inlet, you can see the grave of Kleóboulos, a small round mausoleum from the Hellenistic era. The sea is to the east, and to the west, directly beneath the mountain, the roofs of Líndos can be seen. *April to Oct. 12.30 pm–6.40 pm, Tues–Sun 8.00 am–6.40 pm, in winter Tues–Sun 8.30 am–3 pm; admission 1,200 Dr*

Stairs to the Líndos acropolis

Captain houses

Architecturally a successful combination of elements from Arabia, Byzantine, Egypt and Líndos itself – you can see how far sailors of the 17th century travelled on their long voyages and how many riches they amassed, unhindered and even promoted by the Turkish occupiers. The natural port of Líndos, once filled with ships of wealthy captains, is today economically insignificant. Only yachts and fishing boats rock in the jetty.

The courtyards of captains' houses are, as with many church forecourts, almost always inlaid with *kochláki* mosaics made from black-and-white pebbles – a technique that can be traced back to ancient times. Popular themes were stags and does, the heraldic animals of Rhodes, as well as geometric patterns. The largest room of the house, the *sála*, was always located next to the entrance. The whole entire family slept in this room, and it was also where guests were received.

The walls of the *sála* are adorned with precious, painted ceramic plates. The oldest are those that the sailors brought back from Turkey. At a later time, potters from Líndos created the famous "Líndos plates". They were not intended to be used as crockery, but rather as wall decorations. For this reason, they are equipped with eyelets on the reverse, so that they can be hung from a single nail. Modern versions are made in a ceramics studio and are sold in souvenir shops. A large number of old houses are open to the public, and many of them can be rented as holiday apartments.

Kleóboulos Tomb

The rotunda on the promontory north-east of the bay of Líndos originates from the Hellenistic era. It measures 9 m in diameter and is carefully joined together with hewn stones, without any mortar. In about one hour, a narrow path through completely unspoilt nature leads you there. The path begins at the Palestra restaurant on the northern edge of the main shore of Líndos. You'll pass an old windmill on the way.

Church of the Virgin Mary

The main church of Líndos is worth seeing, especially on account of its 80 frescoes. In fact, the entire church is a huge religious story in pictures. It lies at the centre of the village. The footpath to the acropolis passes it. From above, the domed building resembles a cross. The chancel appears on the ground plans as a protrusion over the crossbeam.

The church was constructed in the 15th century. The black-and-white pebble floor bears a simple wave pattern. The frescoes were painted by an artist from the neighbouring island of Sími. The entire west wall is taken up with a depiction showing the many figures of the Last Judgement. The purpose of this painting is to remind the congregation as they leave the church of the rewards they will receive for leading a pious life, and of the punishments that will befall sin-

St Christophorus in Líndos

ners. The longitudinal walls of the church nave are divided into four rows. The saints can be seen at the bottom, among them a certain St Christophorus who has a dog's head. Above this, the Akathist hymnal is illustrated, a liturgical chant from the 16th century. The Virgin Mary is exalted in the chant's 24 verses.

Above this, the 20 most important church festivals are illustrated, including the Raising of Lazarus, the Entry into Jerusalem, the Crucifixion and Resurrection of Christ, and the Appearances.

The illustrations of the Book of Genesis seen in the top row are especially interesting and intelligible to laypersons. These illustrations depict the creation of the world, the animals, Adam (the first human) and Eve, who was made from one of Adam's ribs.

The church also houses a small museum that is worth a visit only if you are particularly interested in liturgical garments or old books.

Theatre

At the base of the acropolis are the remains of the theatre that was once part of the ancient city. Twenty-seven rows of stone seats can still be discerned. The theatre was built in 4 BC and accommodated some 2,000 spectators.

RESTAURANTS

Food in Líndos is somewhat more expensive than in other places – the advantage being that restaurants are more stylishly furnished and, for the most part, the food tastes very good. You can tell from looking at the menu that Líndos is a British tourist stronghold. Sadly, originality is not one of the strong points of the restaurateurs and bar owners here. Every year, they follow the latest trend: sometimes restaurants with roof terraces are in, sometimes small bars with "original *kochláki*" courtyards are suddenly popular. You will be even less likely to find the same restaurant and/or pub on your next holiday to Líndos than in other areas, with the exception of a few quasi "established" addresses.

Archontiko

Tasteful restaurant with creative Greek and Mediterranean cuisine, located in an old captain house dating from 1605. From the roof terrace, there's a nice view of the acropolis and the ocean. *Odós Apostólou Pávlou; Tel. 31992; category 3*

Cyprus Tavern Timi's Place

Cypriot proprietor Efthímios and his wife (a native of Rhodes) serve Greek and Cypriot specialities in an old Líndos house. You can choose to enjoy your meal inside or on the roof garden. The flag on the roof recalls the Turkish occupation of 40 per cent of Cyprus. *Odós Akropóleos; Tel. 31539; category 2*

Grill on the Hill
This relatively new restaurant has already made a good impression on the locals. Here international cuisine is served and a view of Líndos bay can be admired. *Platía Eleftherías (at the town entrance); Tel. 31834; category 2*

Maria's
Unpretentious, established *tavérna* in the upper area of the town. No view, but very good Greek cooking. *Odós Apostólou Pávlou; Tel. 31375; category 2*

Mavríkos
You can end your day here in an atmospheric way, with busses and taxis nearby. The restaurant is located right at the town's entrance. The dining room is reminiscent of an old cellar, but you're also welcome to sit on the pleasant terrace. The restaurant serves Greek meat and fish specialities, such as lamb chops and sword fish filets. *Platía Eleftherías; Tel. 31232; category 2*

Symposium
A gourmet temple in a restored old house in the centre of town. Good Greek and international dishes are served here. Specialities include steaks and exquisite seafood, such as lobster, and there are reasonably priced meat and fish dishes as well. *Odós Apostólou Pávlou; Tel. 31260; category 2*

Triton
If a long walk on the main beach of Líndos has whet your appetite, you don't have to go very far to satisfy it. In this

Something to enjoy every evening on Rhodes: dining outdoors, under the stars

open-air tavern, fresh fish is served in the afternoons and evenings, and you can choose from meat and pasta, or if you want just a light meal, order a Greek salad. Freshly squeezed fruit juices and cocktails are served at the bar, which is decorated with a *kochláki* mosaic. *Tel. 31222; category 2*

SHOPPING

It's not an exaggeration to say that Líndos is one giant shopping arcade during the summer season. Costume jewellery, silver filigree work, ceramics, rugs, gaudy T-shirts, clothes in folklore style – the selection is vast and you might ask yourself whether you're getting your money's worth at the countless shops and stalls on the right and left sides of the street. Don't worry, on some days, roughly 10,000 people are herded through Líndos, and almost everyone buys something, even if it's only a little souvenir, simply because looking around the shops in the atmospheric surrounding is really enjoyable. If you are considering a large purchase, be sure to think it over first. You might be able to find it in Rhodes city, where many things are less expensive and you might be able to save some money.

There are several supermarkets in the vicinity. At "Lindos", for example, you can look through the numerous shelves while walking on mosaic floors. An advantage is that you can shop late at night for a bottle of wine, some fruit, or maybe even a croissant.

HOTELS

It is useless to recommend the restored old houses that today serve as holiday apartments. They are almost completely under the control of tour operators (mostly from Great Britain) and, at best, can be rented only for a couple of days during the off-peak season. But even that is worthwhile. You can inquire about rentals at the following travel and tour agencies in Líndos village: *Pallas Travel; Tel. 31494; Fax 31595; Savaidis Travel; Tel. 31347; Fax 31451.*

Electra

Guest house with garden, terrace and communal kitchen. *11 rooms with and without shower/ WC. On the road to Pállas beach; Tel. 31266; category 2*

Katholiki

Guest house in a 350-year-old house, nice courtyard and roof terrace. *On the road to Pállas beach; Tel. 31445; category 3*

Líndos Mare

Furnished major hotel with a terrace overlooking Vlícha bay and a freshwater swimming pool, about 3 km away from the town of Líndos. *123 rooms; Tel. 31130; Fax 31131; www.helios.gr/hotels/lindosmare; category 3*

Líndos Village

The hotel and bungalow "village" on Vlícha bay, 5 km north of Líndos, looks like a miniature version of an old, long-established village: white houses nestled into a hill, arcades, two small towers – a relatively large hotel broken down into manageable complexes. The hotel is run by the management of an airline carrier, LTU, a dedicated member of the LTI group. You can book a room at an all-inclusive rate that includes all meals and beverages (non-alcoholic and alcoholic). *186 rooms; Tel. 32000; Fax 31062; category 1*

SPORTS & LEISURE

You can rent pedal boats on Líndos's main beach. Water-skiers can hire equipment at the rental station behind the excursion boats on Pallas beach. On Vlícha beach, 5 km north of Líndos, there are additional water-sport stations located at large hotels which offer water-skiing, para-gliding and other outdoor sports equipment.

ENTERTAINMENT

The narrow streets are full of life until midnight, when the souvenir shops are still open. Music rings out from the pubs. After midnight the jukeboxes are silenced and only quiet fun is permitted. The residents of Líndos need their sleep. At 8 am the next morning, the hustle and bustle (and money-making) starts all over again. If you're a night owl that wants to keep dancing after midnight, you only have to walk a little way – namely towards the beach where music can't disturb the sleepers. Another way to end the evening is with a midnight cocktail, maybe in the same bar where you have breakfast in the morning. In Líndos, many bars close only for a short time between 3 am and 8 am. Live Greek music, which is often danced to, is heard every evening in the Kyriakos *tavérna* on Pallas beach.

Acropolis

Have you ever danced to a hot rhythm outside in the open air, under a pergola? You can finally give it a try in this disco, which is also popular among the young people of Líndos and its environs. It is located on the road to the beach, right next to a restaurant of the same name. For those times when it's necessary to take a break from dancing, you can visit one of the three bars. *Odós Kleovoúlou; Tel. 31391; category 2*

Líndos by night

A bar on three different floors. From the roof terrace, there's an especially pretty view of the roofs of the village, the acropolis and the ocean. *On the same street as the post office; Tel. 31463; category 2*

SURROUNDING AREA

Asklipión (Asklipeion) (107/D3)

★ This little village in the interior of the island (pop. 300) has not really been affected by tourism. The "attractions" are the ruins of a castle that once belonged to the Knights of St John of Jerusalem and the Church of the Dormition of the Virgin Mary (*Kímissi tis Theotókou*). The castle, which was probably built in the 15th century, overlooks the village and affords a nice view. The church of the Virgin Mary dates from the 13th or 14th century, and

View of the interior of the Byzantine Church of the Virgin Mary

additions were added to it later. In the 17th century, the entire church was beautifully painted with frescoes, some of which were restored at the beginning of the 20th century. In addition to depictions of the life of Jesus Christ and the Virgin Mary, there are rare illustrations of Revelation (the Apocalypse). For example, the "Seven Horsemen of the Apocalypse" and the antichrist rising from the depths of the earth. The iconostasis is particularly glorious.

There are two museums near the church that are worth visiting: the first is the Sacral Museum, which displays several icons and old Gospels; the second is the local history museum, housing an interesting collection of agricultural devices *(both open daily 9 am–5 am; admission 300 Dr)*

If you'd like to spend the night in a peaceful mountain village, accommodation can be found in Asklipión. Over the Agapitos Taverna, above the church, there are five modest but clean rooms that can be rented for a very reasonable price. The rooms are perfect for an in-between overnight trip *(Tel. 47255; category 3).*

Gennádi(on) (107/D4)
Shortly before reaching Gennádi, the booming hotel development of the east coast comes to an end. It's still only halfway to Gennádi, but there are *tavérnas* and bars. You can also spend the night in one of three modernized traditional farmhouses.

Glístra Beach (107/E3)
This sandy beach can easily be seen from the coast road between Lárdos and Kiotári and is shaped like a sickle. It is still completely unspoilt.

Ipsenís Convent (107/E2)
The small white convent west of Lárdos is not the most inter-

esting site on the island. It was built in the 19th century, and the bell tower was added in the 1960s. A trip there is still worthwhile, however, because the path there leads through olive groves and pine forests. The nuns are hospitable and the atmosphere of the convent is profoundly peaceful. You can experience the surroundings more indepth by climbing up the small hill next to the convent by way of the pilgrimage path, with its stations of the cross.

A children's home is also part of the convent. The nuns look after children from eastern European countries who are invited by the Orthodox church to spend their vacation there. A big festival is celebrated at the convent every year, on 23 August. On that day, up to 5,000 people stream into the area to celebrate. *Daily 8 am–12.30 pm and 4 pm–6.30 pm*

Kiotári (107/D3)

If you drive south on the coast road, about 5.5 km past the turn-off to the Ágios Vassílios church, you'll arrive at an intersection. Turn left onto the small streets and drive until you reach the fishing village, with its pretty, pebbled beach. Some years ago, the village was almost like paradise. That's now long gone, however, since large hotels are being built on the section of the coast between Lárdos and Kiotári. A large mass is conducted annually on 6 August in Kiotári's village church, which is dedicated to the transfiguration of Christ (*Metamorphosis*).

The *Kiotari Watersports Centre* at the Hotel Rodos Maris *(Tel. 47000)* will delight those who like water sports. It offers surfing courses and sailing lessons on DART-18 catamarans, as well as a comprehensive water-skiing training programme, including knee and wakeboards.

Lachaniá (106/C5)

The small beach village is the only place on the west coast that hasn't yet been hit by mass tourism. Several old houses have been lovingly restored by resident foreigners, so that the old village atmosphere has been maintained as best as possible. Individualists can stay here in private rooms and historic village houses. The mayor, who owns the Horizon Taverna (*Tel. 46033*), and the village priest, who is also the proprietor of the Acropol chez Chrissis (*Tel. 46032*) Taverna across the street can both supply you with information about accommodation. One of the best island *tavérnas* is located at the church square at the lower edge of the village: Plátanos Taverna (*Tel. 46027; category 3*).

Láerma (107/D1)

The village (pop. 650) lies almost exactly in the centre of the island, among olive groves and corn fields. All the villages in the surrounding area are at least 11 km away from one another. A dozen tourists drive through the village each day on their way to nearby Thári Monastery. We highly recommend stopping at the *Bella Vista Grill House* and having a cup of coffee or trying a very good marc schnapps called *zoúma*. The hospitable owner, Stérgos, or his son Geórgios sit and tell their infrequent guests stories about Vassílis, the third son, who has been living in Germany for more than 30 years.

Láerma is a "typical Greek" village. There are no souvenir shops since tourists come here so rarely. There is not even a *tavérna* with "traditional Greek food", only a couple of *kafenías* where you can order a snack to eat. Towards Asklipión, there's a beautiful footpath (about 11 km) that wends its way through virtually unspoilt countryside.

Lárdos **(107/E2)**

The black granite that is typical of the island appears very frequently in these parts. Therefore, it has the same name as this small, very green and still relatively intact village. It's only in recent years that blocks of apartments and small hotels have been built here. Large hotels have emerged on nearby beaches. Tourists who wish to experience the daily life of the Greek village with their own eyes will feel at home in Lárdos – if their first priority isn't shopping. There are some nice *kafenías* and *tavérnas* offering good, plain cooking, located in the village square. Lárdos is about 2.5 km away from two nice beaches. You can stay overnight, for example in the modest hotel *Fédra (11 rooms; Tel. 44218; category 2)*.

Plimmíri **(106/C5)**

This tiny hamlet is the port of Lachaniá village. From here, a mostly isolated pebbly beach stretches out for more than 1 km towards the south. Today, a *tavérna* takes up part of the very simple monastery that was established in 1837. Many fragments of a large early Christian basilica were used again to build the well-preserved church. Capitals from ancient columns that were found in the immediate vicinity were also used during the construction of the church. This helps to prove that a small city must have existed here during Antiquity.

Thári Monastery **(107/D2)**

This monastery, located in a forest near Láerma, was empty for a long time, and occupied by monks again as late as the 1990s. It has become the centre of a revival of the monastic way of life on Rhodes. Its abbot, formerly active in Kenya as a missionary, is the unofficial candidate for the highest church office in the Orthodoxy, the Patriarchy in Constantinople. The monastery broadcasts its own radio and television programmes, takes care of children from all over the world in its holiday resorts and sends priests to village churches where no more church services are being conducted.

Some of the monastery's more than 20 frescoes date from the 14th century. They depict saints and early fathers of the church, as well as scenes from the life of Christ and the Virgin Mary, among them Jesus healing the blind, the lame and lepers, as well as the Last Supper. The illustration of Christ in the chancel is rarely found in Orthodox churches: Christ enthroned as ruler of the world. The square frame, symbolizing the universe is – also a rarity in Greece – supported by the four symbols of the Evangelists. The angel represents Matthew, the eagle symbolizes John, the lion stands for Mark and the bull for Luke.

PÉFKI

(107/F3) There were only a few summer houses in the 1970s. Thanks to tourism, a village has emerged that comes alive during the tourist season. Péfki is perfect for a holiday at the seaside and as a place to come for a side trip. Its biggest attractions are the sandy beach and many small swimming inlets. Even more apartment complexes, hotels, shops, restaurants and snack bars are emerging on the right and left sides of the relatively seldom driven road from Líndos to Lárdos. The shopping area is not yet nice enough for a long stroll, but nightlife is slowly coming to life. The hotels try to make up for this by offering many kinds of parties, Greek evenings and *karaoke nights* for people who are staying at the hotel as well as for guests from outside. Unfortunately, there's not much of an opportunity to meet any locals from Péfki who are neither waiters nor souvenir vendors.

RESTAURANTS

Greek House
A purely family operation not far from Péfka beach. Owner Fédra does the cooking herself: stuffed *chtapódi* (octopus), rich *moussaká* (pasta bake with aubergine and minced meat), roasted lamb with aromatic garlic sauce. *Tel. 44317; category 2*

Tsambíkos
This restaurant can be seen from afar because it is located on a hill in the centre of town, high above all its competitors on the

The Apostle Paul is alleged to have come ashore here, between Líndos and Péfki

street and beach below. The kitchen serves up Greek and international specialities ranging from stuffed tomatoes to filet mignon, and offers such high quality that it's very hard to get a place on the large terrace during the summer months. There's a large selection of Greek wines to choose from to accompany your meal – and you'll receive a complimentary view overlooking the roofs of Péfki, one that is dream-like in the moonlight. *Tel. 48240; category 2*

HOTELS

Illission

Coming from Líndos, the long, three-storeyed new building is located at the end of the village, set back a little from the road. It's only a few steps from there to a clean beach, but one that is rocky in some areas. In spite of its large size, the hotel, opened in 1991, is still family-like. Owners Kóstas and Caterína Kóntos like to sit together with their guests at the bar or on the terrace. Kóstas continues to work in the afternoons as a teacher (Greek, history) at a secondary school in Rhodes city. The hotel has modern rooms, mini-apartments and suites; almost all have a balcony or terrace and an ocean view. There is a snack bar, a restaurant, tennis courts and miniature golf courses as well as a swimming pool with a paddling pool for children. *70 rooms; Tel. 48150; Fax 48148; category 2*

Sunrise

This hotel, which opened in 1998, is located directly above a small, flat sloping beach. During the tourist season, it offers its guests 62 air-conditioned rooms and apartments, which are equipped with refrigerators and televisions, but can be reserved only with half-board. There's a nice swimming pool (with a children's pool) and a pool bar. Part of the restaurant is reserved for non-smokers. Additional amenities include a tennis court and a small supermarket. *On the shore road; Tel. 48311; Fax 48345; category 1*

SPORTS & LEISURE

Bicycling

Good quality bicycles can be rented pretty much everywhere – exactly the right transportation for the long distances in the sprawling village or for an excursion to Líndos.

Water sports

There are surfboards to be found, for example at the St George Club. The hotel is located at the entrance to the town, as can be seen from Lárdos. Sports facilities (tennis, etc.) are available to everyone. *On the shore road; Tel. 48311; Fax 48345; category 1*

ENTERTAINMENT

Sail Inn Cocktail Bar

There's a nice view of Péfki from the terrace. There is also an air-conditioned interior room. Snacks and beverages are served. Once a week, the proprietor puts on a Greek night with dances you can join in on. *In the town centre; Tel. 44248*

Mountains, valleys and coasts

Deep-blue water and white marble, majestic fortresses and secluded monasteries – many paths to hidden beauty

The sign on the arrivals terminal of the airport (as ugly as most other airports) greets visitors with "Welcome to the island of the sun". Planes depart and land by the minute, a queue of pale newcomers stand in front of customs, while a cluster of tanned people look for the "Departures" sign. It's peak tourist season. The next stop: a ride in a tour bus heading in the direction of the city of Rhodes that passes by quite unappealing beaches and large hotels.

This is how many tourists first encounter Rhodes. Fortunately, the island has much more to offer than this first impression. Once you get to know Rhodes, you will know the many faces of Greece: the grey, fast-paced modern big city, loud and hectic, but carefree; the barren, sunburnt profile of the summer scenery; majestic forests; cool valleys filled with springs and cheerful voices; boats rocking gently in the harbour and fishermen repairing their nets on the jetty; noisy beaches; ancient marble under the glowing sun, accompanied by a concert of cicadas; chapels nestled between cypress trees; whitewashed houses on narrow lanes and women chatting on the front steps, crochet work in hand.

A vestige of Byzantium: the Church of Ágios Nikólaos Fountoukli

If you want to, you can see all these faces in a single day. But you should really give yourself more time. A round-trip around the island is about 220 km long. The northern landscape is gently rolling, green and inviting. On the east coast, there are long stretches of sandy beaches, with small bays that are encircled by trees. Faliráki, a town perfect for swimming and leisure activities, is located there.

In contrast, the west coast is virtually unspoilt. The beaches there are some what shorter and more rocky, the wind is stronger and the coast is steeper. The west coast is for individualists and will most

MARCO POLO SELECTION: ON AND AROUND RHODES

1 Alimniá
More goats than residents – there are still isolated beaches here (page 86)

2 Wedding in Archángelos
Experience Greek hospitality and *joie de vivre* (page 80)

3 Kámiros
The Pompeii of Rhodes offers beautiful views of the country and the sea, interesting insights into city life of 2000 years ago and fish specialities in Kámiros Skála (page 85)

likely remain the east coast's "poor sister" for a long time to come. The ruins of the city of Kámiros are located here, and the western half of the island boasts the three highest mountains, Profítis Ilías (798 m), Akramítis (825 m) and Atáviros (1,215 m).

Towards the south, the island becomes more barren and rugged, typical of the Aegean region. In summer it is dominated by dusty earth tones, strong white sunlight and black shadows. Landscape that fascinates, but only tempts a few into staying. Therefore, the Gennádi – Kattaviá – Apolakkiá triangle is almost unknown territory among tourists.

Many monasteries, churches and chapels dot the landscape – places that are rarely overcrowded. You can often find yourself alone with the austere faces of the saints that are depicted on the icons. Places filled with burning oil lamps, candles in flat containers filled with sand and solitude, or with brownish stone walls, arcades and leftover ruins of modest Byzantine buildings. Even though Rhodes is no longer a white spot on the map, it is still an island that is well worth exploring.

AFÁNTOU

(103/E4) The name originates from *áfanton*, meaning invisible. In fact, the village cannot be seen from the sea. There is a historical reason for this, of course. The ancient settlement on the coast was destroyed by Saracen pirates back in the seventh century. In order to ensure against any future attacks, the surviving residents built new houses further inland.

At first glance, the "invisible" village is quite nondescript and thus not overcrowded by tourists. Instead of the same old tourist monotony, you can experience a piece of authentic rural life in this village. The town of Afántou has a very special relationship with Germany: in the 1960s, a handful of people from Afántou moved to a German industrial city. Today, at least a thousand men and women from Afántou still supposedly live there. The 5,350 residents of Afántous live primarily from selling beautiful ceramics and rugs.

A tip: Not every place that includes Afántou in it's name is located here! However, such places are never so far away that you couldn't walk there. From Afántou, you can take a municipal bus to get to both the city of Rhodes and Faliráki.

MUSEUM

To call it a "museum" is perhaps a little too exaggerated for this exhibition of sacral objects and secular arts and crafts from the Byzantine era. The exhibition is located next to the church. *Daily 9 am–12 am and 3 pm–5 pm; admission 300 Dr*

RESTAURANTS

There are several modest *tavérnas* and snack bars in the village, as well as cafeterias (where young people get together) and a couple of traditional *kafenías.*

Golfer

Restaurant and café located across from the golf course, on the main street. Good Greek cooking is served here. *Tel. 518 61; category 2*

SHOPPING

Ancient art

This pottery studio specializes in vases and plates that are painted in Classical styles. Crockery and traditional Rhodes wall plates in a large variety of styles are sold as well. An old potter demonstrates the work on a foot-operated potter's wheel – it's just a shame that as soon as he's finished, he moulds the unique piece of art back into a lump of clay for the next demonstration. *On the coast road in the direction of Líndos; Tel. 514 86 or 517 85*

HOTELS

Oásis

A hotel and bungalow complex that is somewhat hidden between splendid, shady trees, but about 1 km away from the Afántou pebble beach. For this reason, there's a swimming pool surrounded by the tables and chairs of the café. You can choose between apartments for two to four people, bungalows and double rooms in the hotel. There's also a playground on the grounds. The "oasis" is ideal for families with small children and, owing to its out-of-the-way location (there's a path to Afántou that you can walk in 15 minutes), for Rhodian holidaymakers who want a little peace and quiet. *Somewhat set back from the coast road; 37 rooms; Tel. 517 71; Fax 517 70; www.rodosnet.gr/antonios/index.html; category 2*

Philoxénia

The pretty Greek name of this apartment complex signifies "hospitality". The six modest studios, each for two persons, are located on a quiet side street. They include a room that doubles as both a living room and bedroom and an integrated kitchenette, as well as a shower and WC. Fresh linens are delivered once a week and housekeeping is conducted twice a week (included in room rate). Afántou beach is about 2 km away. *Tel. 510 83; no fax; category 3*

SPORTS & LEISURE

The kilometre-long pebble beach of Afántou, the gently sloping coast and the clear water guarantee pure swimming for both adults and children. Except for pedal boat rentals, there are only a few organized water sports.

Rhodes' only golf course (18 holes) is located east of the coast road; the entrance is well-marked by signs and guests are welcome. *Tel. 514 51*

SURROUNDING AREA

Agía Triáda (103/D4)
The one-naved, barrel-vaulted church at Psínthos, dedicated to the Holy Trinity, originated in the 14th century. Most of the approximately 20 restored frescoes depict the life of Christ. A holy shrine had already been erected here in Antiquity, and an early Christian church was built later on this site. Part of the structure was used again by the master builder Agía Triáda, as was customary then.

Katholikí Afántou (103/E4)
This small church was built over many centuries. The frescoes here merit a visit, even though art historians do not assess them to be of any great value. To get

Waterfall at Petaloúdes

to the church, coming from the direction of the city of Rhodes, you have to drive past the site. Shortly after the "Afantou Golf" sign, you'll see a sign for "Afantou Beach" on the left. Turn off there; the church is located on the left side, on the road to the beach.

Petaloúdes (Butterfly Valley) (102/C3)
In former times, hundreds of thousands of butterflies (in Greek: *petaloúdes)* fluttered around the 5-km-long valley. They were mostly lured by the scent of the amber trees, outside Rhodes, are found only in Asia Minor. The unfortunate reason why the orange and black "Spanish Flags" (scientific name *Callimorpha quadripunctaria)* haven't come around anymore for many years: bus loads full of clapping and yelling tourists. To protect the butterflies, the valley has at least been reduced to a public pathway of 1 km. Supposedly, there are

even bigger butterfly swarms found on other parts of Rhodes – fortunately, no tourist guides have revealed any more details. The stream, which is full of water all-year round, makes this valley a small paradise. In the peak of summer, you can walk through the luxuriant green and feel the cool breeze. *Open daily 9 am–5 pm; admission 600 Dr*

Psínthos **(103/D4)**
A green and still today "Greek" village. For the inhabitants of Rhodes, Psínthos is a village steeped in history. In 1912, the Italians conquered the Turks and gained control of Rhodes. It took more than another 30 years before the island became Greek.

You can eat very good in the *tavérnas* in the village square. There are also private rooms. The surrounding area is good for hiking and bicycling. There are small churches worth seeing, especially in the area around Maritsá.

APOLAKKIÁ

(106/B3) The coast between Apolakkiá and Kattaviá is a piece of unspoilt landscape: long, often empty sandy beaches, dunes, low brushwood on a rocky ground – not even a village nearby. It's almost a tourist no-man's-land here: just the right excursion for someone who wants to be alone with sea and nature and is happy to do without the comforts of urban life.

The relatively big (by Greek standards) mountain village of Apolakkiá (pop. 600) has only started to be affected by mass tourism in recent years. Daily life still runs at its own leisurely pace, however. People primarily earn their living from cultivating grains, watermelon and honeydew melons. The few tourists who spend their entire holiday here in the southern part of the island are for the most part regular visitors and for years have stayed in the same modest room owned by the same proprietor. If you don't need a swimming paradise at your feet (the rocky beach is 3 km away), but valuable time spent with the locals, this is the place for you. There are several *tavérnas* with good old plain Greek cooking, located in the vicinity.

SIGHTS

Ágios Geórgios o Wárdas
The one-naved chapel is located in a clearing some 4 km north of Apolakkiá. Follow the road towards Gennádi until you reach the end of the village and from there turn left at the first sign that says "Dam". After about 2 km, you'll cross a bridge and shortly afterwards, turn left on-to a country lane. From there, it's only about 100 m until you will see the chapel located on your right. We recommend that you take a hike along this stretch, especially if you are there in spring, when the island is covered in green. The frescoes in the church are some of the oldest on Rhodes. They date back to the time the church was built, the late 13th century. The paintings depict scenes from the life of Christ in addition to illustrations of the

Virgin Mary and several saints, among them, of course, St George, to whom the church is dedicated.

HOTEL

Amalia

Ideal for "motorized" holiday-makers with a car or motorbike who are looking for a hotel in a rustic area. All 18 rooms have balconies, and there is a small, nice pool as well. *On the village square; Tel. 613 65; Fax 613 77; category 3*

SURROUNDING AREA

Atáviros (105/F3)

If you climb up Rhodes's highest mountain (1,215 m), you will be rewarded with wonderful views of the entire island. If the weather is good, you can even see Crete on the horizon. Starting from the mountain village of Émbonas, the climb takes about four hours, including breaks. You have to be sure to wear hiking gear (long trousers, boots, sun hat) and take refreshments with you (don't forget to bring plenty of water!). And remember, never hike alone! Several hikers have had accidents. The climb can be dangerous, especially on cloudy days because the fog gets thicker as you get closer to the top. The best time to climb the mountain is in spring, when the meadows are in full bloom.

Émbonas (105/F3)

This village on the slopes of Atáviros is a standard part of the island tour and is an extremely popular destination for organized Greek evenings. However, it's not really worth visiting since the old village centre can hardly be recognized anymore in view of all the new construction. At best, it's worthwhile to stop at the modern Emery wine cellars *(at the entrance to the village; Mon–Fri 9 am–3.20 pm, during the peak season, daily 9 am–4.30 pm),* where you can indulge in some wine-tasting – however you can do so only while standing up.

Kattaviá (106/B5)

The southernmost village of the island lies in a wide plain (in the peak of summer, it resembles the steppe), in which the Italians set up a landing strip during World War II, and which is today primarily used for growing grain and melons. The atmosphere in this sleepy village seems almost North African. The *tavérnas* in the shady village square earn their money almost solely from tourists. The cross-shaped domed church, consecrated to the Dormition of the Virgin Mary, contains frescoes from the 16th to the 19th century, but is closed most of the time. Visitors can spend the night at the small Prassoníssi Club Hotel *(17 rooms; Tel. 912 31; category 1).* The most recommended *tavérna* is *I Kattaviá (Tel. 912 85; category 3).*

Mesanagrós (106/B4)

It seems like the clocks must have stopped here shortly after the end of World War II. The some 60 residents of this village in the Koukoúliari mountains live in traditional one-room houses. The steep streets are wide enough for only two loaded-up mules walking side by side. If you are travelling with a car, it's best to leave it at the entrance to the village.

You hardly see any young people around here, for most of them have moved to the city of Rhodes or to one of the up-and-coming holiday resorts on the east coast. The older people have stayed and are happy to meet anyone who wants to sit and chat a bit with them while having a cup of *métrio* in the *kafeníon*.

The village church of Mesanagrós is consecrated to the Dormition of the Virgin Mary *(Kímissi tis Theotóku)* and stands on the ruins of a church dating from the early Christian period. You can also easily identify the rest of the ancient columns. Church services are held here only twice a year, on the 15 and 23 August, when the Dormition of the Virgin Mary is celebrated. If you'd like to visit the church, the key is hanging in the *kafeníon*.

The village's only "restaurant" is the *Café O Mike (category 3)*. Simple dishes, such as fried eggs or Greek salad, are on the menu. If you wish to stay overnight in Mesanagrós, enquire in the café about getting a private room.

About 3.5 km south of the village, alongside the road to Lachaniá, lies the Ágios Thomás chapel. The biggest religious holiday celebrated here is "Thomas Sunday", held on the Sunday after Easter Sunday. On the day before the holiday, a much-visited festival is held in front of the church, beneath the old cypress trees.

Monólithos **(106/A2)**

The 240-m-high "Single Rock" (a translation of the name) rises up out of the landscape like an enormous stony finger. In the 15th century, the Knights of St John presumably built a fortress on the plateau *(always open to the public)*. The walls (one of which is dedicated to St George), the now whitewash-

Monólithos, a rocky outcrop in the vast countryside

ed chapel and a couple of remains have been preserved. The climb up is made via narrow stony steps. It's best to come shortly before sunset and enjoy the view of the sea. You can see Cape Foúrni to the south, Cape Armenistís to the north-west and, far into the ocean, the island of Chálki.

The village of Monólithos, located about 2 km away, is "invisible" from the sea, just as Afántou is. This was advantageous, because in earlier times, it protected the inhabitants from pirate attacks. Only about 500 old people live there now, and the village is slowly dying out. The school had to be closed in 1990. The beaches, small bays between cliffs, can be easily reached on foot, by moped or by taking the recently built paved road that leads directly there – nonetheless they are still rarely visited.

Prassoníssi (106/A–B6)

Prassoníssi is actually the name of a small, uninhabited island located off the southern tip of Rhodes. In the meantime, people use the name for the several-hundred-metre-wide and several kilometre-long sandy beaches on the southern tip itself. Because it extends both the west and east, it offers ideal windsurfing conditions. Most people bring their boards with them, despite the fact that there's been a surfing school here since 1999. If you can't find a vacant room, you can camp out in the dunes. The rubbish from the beachgoers, the flotsam and jetsam that washes ashore as well as the clumps of tar do not help make Prassoníssi into a beach paradise, in spite of its scenic beauty. Things are looking up, though. Two guest houses and three *tavérnas* have cropped up, and more are in the works. Especially recommended is the *Taverne Lighthouse*, which serves goat chops and homemade pork sausages as specialities. There is a guest house above the *tavérna* run by a Swiss-Greek couple who rent out 19 rooms *(Tel. 910 30; Fax 919 13; category 3)*.

Siánna (105/D4)

The small village on Mt. Akramítis has been only moderately affected by tourism. Groups on a tour of the island who take their lunch break here stay only as long as it takes to eat, have coffee and take a tour through the steep, narrow streets. For those interested in art history, the village offers a – in comparison to the size of the village – giant church dating from the 19th century, which is consecrated to St Panteléimon, as well the ruins of a fortress built by the Knights of St John on a hill above the village. A culinary speciality of Siánna is yoghurt, which you can buy there, for example at the Taverne Village Place *(category 3)*. The proprietor also serves and sells a kind of marc schnapps that is called *zoúma* on Rhodes, which brings tears to the eyes of many people on the first swallow –

especially if you drink it without chilling it first. Located directly across from the church square: a cosy old *kafeníon* that also serves as a small shop selling assorted wares, as was common in former times in Greek villages. *Zoúma* is less expensive here than it is anywhere else.

Skiádi Monastery **(106/B4)**
This monastery, looked after by monks from Thári, is famous because the Icons of Panagía (Virgin of Mary) Skiadiní, the most valuable ones on Rhodes, are kept there. The monastery can be reached from Mesanagrós or the coastal road. It was built in the 14th century. In the 19th century, the small monastery church was built into the new big church as a chancel. The famous icon on the iconostasis cannot be missed: gilded and embossed silver metal covers the figures of the Virgin Mary and the infant Jesus, except for their faces and throats. In the weeks leading up to Easter, the icon is taken for one or more days to the surrounding villages and the neighbouring island of Chálki, in accordance with a very precise plan. Since the icons are thought to work miracles, pilgrims, mostly women, come to the monastery the whole year round.

ARCHÁNGELOS

(103/D5-6) The second-largest city on Rhodes (a population of almost 6,000 – in Greece, any location with a population of 5,000 or more is designated a city) proves that tourism is not synonymous with the disappearance of a large part of what makes a city fascinating: old, whitewashed houses, bumpy roads, people with more time than the tourists seem to have. For a few years now, German and Dutch visitors in particular have been

Light and shade in Archángelos

coming in droves to visit the "archangel" city (a translation of the name "Archángelos"). Almost all the hotels are located in the modern area of the city. You can only rent apartments and private rooms in the historic centre. Holiday guests in the "old" Archángelos just liven up the city a little – and put money in the cash registers of the souvenir shops. Children in blue school uniforms wait at the bus stop to be taken home to one of the surrounding villages that don't have their own school. Women wearing the traditional head scarf go by at a leisurely pace, bulky shopping bags in hand, and vanish into shops. The shops in Archángelos still look like they did everywhere in Greece 20 years ago: small, understated, dark and jam-packed. For the most part, the selection is greater than you'd expect at first glance. The item the customer is looking for is possibly hidden away in drawers and shoe cartons.

In contrast to many other small villages, Archángelos is very lively. Since they can now live well from tourism, not as many people move away as once did.

★ During the summer, a wedding is held in Archángelos almost every week, with all that is traditionally Rhodes: relatives and friends of the bride-groom pick up the bride from her parent's house in a bridal procession. The musicians lead the procession. A church wedding in accordance with Orthodox rites follows, and then the big open-air celebration begins, complete with music and dancing. Mutton is often roasted on a spit, and the wine flows. For the hospitable inhabitants of Archángelos, it is tradition to invite new friends to the wedding, especially if they are spending their holidays in the village.

Easter is celebrated with particular alacrity in Archángelos. Remember, the Good Friday procession and Resurrection mass don't begin until past midnight.

SIGHTS

Church

Like a snow-white finger wearing glittery rings, the bell tower of the church, dedicated to Michael the Archangel, rises up between the equally white houses of old Archángelos. The neo-Baroque building was a bequest from the Italian occupiers. The church dates from the mid-19th century. The most interesting thing about it is the mosaic (called *kochláki* in Greek) in the courtyard, composed of black-and-white pebbles, as is customary in Rhodes. Owing to the square pattern, the entire building seems to be alienated in its perspective, an effect which offers rich creative opportunities for ambitious photographers. The parish fair is held on 8 November and/or the evening before.

Knights' Fortress

The ✵ ruins of a fortress of the Knights of St John, which Grand Master Orsini had built in the mid-15th century, are located on a hill on the edge of the city. Near the entrance, several coats of arms, among them the Orsini coat of arms dated 1467 – the year the building was completed. From the citadel, there is a nice view of the white silhouette of the historic part of the city.

RESTAURANTS

There is a large selection of *tavérnas* and cafés. Many of them are open until late in the evening.

Milano

Don't shy away from eating pizza in Greece. The Italian speciality is very popular with the Greeks, and you can eat in a good pizzeria on the main road towards Rhodes city, which locals certainly frequent. *On the village square; Tel. 225 73; category 2*

SHOPPING

There's a large selection of local arts and crafts in Archángelos. The village residents specialize in weaving and ceramics. The tall, flat-heeled Rhodes leather boots that some women in the village still wear can also be bought here.

Rugs are sold at *Anastássios Saríkas.* The showroom is located across from the bus stop. The rugs are made by weavers who work from home and some of them don't mind at all if an interested visitor takes a look over their shoulders. You can find out some addresses by asking in the Tsambíka Chrístou souvenir shop on the main street *(Tel. 225 00 or 229 62)*. You shouldn't come during the afternoon siesta time, which in summer is from 1 pm to 5 pm. Daughter Cleopatra sells rugs, sweaters and jumpers, as well as other needlework that she openly admits largely comes from northern Greece or Athens. She also procures private rooms.

There are several ceramics studios with large showrooms located along the divided highway that leads from Rhodes to Líndos.

HOTELS

Meandros

This two-storey building lies on a quiet street almost 1 km away from the city centre. The 20 simple rooms with modern amenities can all be reached via the arcade, and all have balconies. There's a small freshwater pool at the hotel. The hotel serves a breakfast buffet, and you can book a room with half-board (dinner) if you'd like. *Tel. 228 96; Fax 238 96; category 2*

Semina

The apartment complex is located in a quiet residential area that's only about 300 m from the city centre. Here visitors can rent studios with living rooms and bedrooms that accommodate two to three persons. The studios also have kitchenettes, showers and WCs, as well as a balcony or terrace. The service includes daily housekeeping and fresh linens twice a week. Guests must arrange for their own meals. *34 apartments; behind the school; Tel. 222 10; category 2*

SURROUNDING AREA

Charáki (107/F1)

Not long ago, there were only a few summer houses on this pebble beach. Many belong to farmers from the inland villages of Malónas and Mássari, where people still earn their living from growing oranges and tangerines. Both of these villages are to be credited for the fact that there are always plenty of this fruit on the island (in his book, *Reflections on a Marine Venus*, Lawrence Durrell called Rhodes the "island of glowing oranges") – even though there isn't enough left over for export.

In the meantime, Charáki has risen to the status of a popular swimming area that doesn't have blocks of hotels, rather, for the most part, people stay in small guest houses and apartment complexes. A car-free beach promenade with cafés, restaurants and bars make the place even more attractive. One of the best and most original fish and seafood restaurants on the island, the Argo *(Tel. 514 10; category 1),* is located on the southern end of the promenade. It spoils its guests with fresh seafood, including rock lobsters from its own tank. The small Ágii Apóstoli chapel at the town square is worth taking a look at. It was painted in the traditional style by artist monks from Mt. Athos in 1997 and 1998.

Féraklos Fortress (107/F1)
The remains of the Féraklos fortress (built in the time of the Knights of St John) lie on a mountain north of Charáki. Most likely, a fortress was located here in Antiquity. It is known for certain that the knights of St John besieged a Byzantine fortress here in 1306. In 1470, Grand Master Orsini had the fortress restored. It was then used as a prison for prisoners of war taken by the Order and as place of exile for knights who had run up too many debts. From the northern side of the mountain, there are nice views of the fertile countryside of Malónas and Mássari and of the bay with a sandy beach at the foot of the mountain. An art-historical treasure is embedded in the rock above the bay: the small Agía Agáthi church carved into the stone. It is thought to date from the 12th or 13th century. Agáthi bay, only about a 30-minute-walk away from the seaside resort of Charáki, offers a pretty, approx. 200-m-long sandy beach, which is usually quite empty. Two refreshment stands have set up tables in the sand; only an abandoned building on the slope mars the beauty of the scene.

Stegná (Stegená) (103/D6)
The out-of-the-way beach village is reached via a tortuous street that leads through the old, almost deserted pottery village of Petróna. The small, sandy beach is not as nice as the one in Tsambíka, but on the other hand, it is greener and you can try out some simple but good Greek food at the shady *tavérna.* Many apartment complexes can be found here, such as *Antonios (8 apartments; Tel. 228 09; Fax 227 79; www.rodosnet.gr/antonios/index.html; category 2).*

FALIRÁKI

(103/E3) Just 25 years ago, there were only a couple of fisherman's cottages and a 6-km-long sandy beach here. Families from the city of Rhodes enjoy coming to Faliráki to swim because the sea is very shallow and therefore "childproof". The first hotels were built in the early 1980s, and today a huge amusement park with water attractions for both children and adults sits on this formerly inconspicuous site, located directly on the east coast road. 20,000 guest beds, fast-food places, bars, discos, fur shops – in short, "the Las Vegas of Rhodes", as one local tourist agency characterized it in its brochure.

Faliráki has little to do with a real Greek village. It resembles a small, bustling city whose residents all have the same "employer" – tourism. In summer, you can hardly see the beach on account of the dense crowds of sweaty sun worshippers.

Faliráki is a holiday resort that is good for people whose primary objective is to have fun and who are not nature-lovers. Children will be able to find playmates of the same age and young people can have fun surfing and water-skiing and going to discos at night. Just remember, however, one thing that Faliráki is not is quiet!

RESTAURANTS

It is quantity rather than quality that characterizes Faliráki's restaurants.

Apollon

In the Apollo Beach Hotel's small snack bar, you can eat an English breakfast or have a light lunch under the trees, and if you've eaten too much, you can just jump into the water a little later. *Tel. 855 13; category 2*

Monaxiá

"Loneliness" is perhaps not the most suitable name anymore for this nondescript beach café at the Sun Palace Hotel. They serve reasonably priced, good fish dishes, and live Greek music is played here two evenings a week. *Tel. 853 07; category 2*

SHOPPING

There are many, many supermarkets and souvenir shops. Since Faliráki is not a long-established village, it is not steeped in the tradition of arts and crafts – to see those you'd be better advised to drive directly to the source in the interior of the island. Faliráki has the advantage of offering you the opportunity to bring home a custom-tailored suit or fur coat from your holiday at the seaside. A tailor can be found, for example, at the Faliraki Beach Hotel *(Tel. 856 68)*.

HOTELS

No other place on Rhodes has so many guest beds in such a small space – unfortunately, "construction atrocities" of the 1960s and 1970s predominate the resort.

Esperos Village

One of the nicest island hotels, it resembles a village because it is located on a slope, high above the bustle of the village. Complimentary bus shuttle to the beach. *210 rooms; Tel. 860 46; Fax 857 41; www.esperia-hotels.gr; category 1*

Liberia

If you're staying in Faliráki and want to find something a little quieter, this hotel (built in 1987) is the right place. It is located on a side street about 800 m from the town centre (sign from the main street: Profítis Ammós). It is about 400 m to the beach. All 75 rooms have a bath and WC. There is a swimming pool, snack bar and tennis court. The almost obligatory Greek evening is held in the hotel on Friday evenings. *Tel. 850 09; no fax; category 2*

Mousses
The small complex (by Faliráki standards) is about a 15-minute walk from the town centre. It's only 200 m from the beach (sand and pebbles). The complex consists of bungalow-type units, most of which are ground-level. There's a bath or a WC and a balcony or terrace in each room. The facility has its own small swimming pool, which all guests are welcome to use. *41 rooms; Tel. 853 03; Fax 856 25; category 2*

SPORTS & LEISURE

During peak season, water sports abound and there's something for everyone: pedal, row and motor boats, jetskis, surfing, parasailing. In addition, you can play tennis or miniature golf. The cheapest form of enjoyment is swimming – that goes for Faliráki as well. The best addresses for organized water sports are the large hotels. The best by far is the one run by Overschmidt International in front of the Colossos Beach Hotel. In addition to renting equipment, you can also take surfing and sailing courses, as well as professional water-skiing lessons. Guided mountain bike tours and bike rentals are offered by Hellas Bike Travel in Grecotel Rhodos Royal.

ENTERTAINMENT

There's not enough time for anyone to get bored in Faliráki. A much more common problem is that visitors go to bed early and can't get any peace and quiet because so much is going on. Music is silenced after midnight in the residential area, but if you're still not tried, you can continue to dance all night in a disco on the beach.

SURROUNDING AREA

Anthony Quinn Bay **(103/E4)**
This small, rocky bay at Ladikó bears this wonderful name because the Greek government gave it to the famous actor as a token of gratitude for shooting the epic film *The Guns of*

Today, even we lesser mortals are allowed to swim in Anthony Quinn Bay

Navarone (Gregory Peck and Irene Papas co-starred with Quinn in the film), thus making the island known to millions. Quinn, as the story goes, stayed with locals the entire time – and at the end of filming, he had mastered the worst Greek swear words. The subsequent democratically elected government, however, took the gift back. Thus, the wonderful bay with its small sandy beach is today open to everyone. *On the coast road to Líndos after driving about 1 km, turn left towards Ladikó; diagonally opposite from Hotel Ladikó, you'll see a gravel road that leads to the bay*

Ladikó **(103/E4)**
It's been only a couple of years since this small village started developing into a seaside resort. The location is ideal for tourists who want peace and quiet, but also a happening beach life. It is, after all, not very far to Faliráki. You can stay very comfortably in the Hotel Cathrin *(159 rooms; Tel. 858 81; Fax 856 24; category 2)*, 650 m from the sandy beach.

KÁMIROS

(102/A3) ★ It's not possible to stay and have your holidays here – the city was never inhabited again after the earthquake in the second century AD. Yet, Kámiros is still the most prominent place on the west coast, and shows one of the island's nicest sides.

SIGHTS

Excavation sites
An advance warning: during the tourist season, the excavation sites are often overflowing with bus loads of people. If you really want to enjoy your tour of the sites, you should start off right when it opens or right before it closes.

Kámiros was the smallest of the three Doric cities and had its heyday in the sixth century BC. It wasn't discovered until the mid-19th century and wasn't excavated until the 1930s, by Italian archaeologists. The city is built on a slope. From the houses, you can see green meadows, pine forests and olive groves, and residents of the upper city had a view of the coast. You can still enjoy this view today – there's not a hotel or industrial plant in sight to obstruct the view.

However, the residents of Kámiros paid a high price for their choice location. In 226 BC, a terrible earthquake destroyed almost all the buildings. Despite this, the people stayed and rebuilt their city. Some 300 years later, in AD 42, another big earthquake hit, levelling Kámiros. This time, nobody wanted to stay – the city was abandoned.

Most of the ruins of the "Pompeii of Rhodes" date from the Hellenistic period. The city ascends in terraces. The lowest terrace was embedded into the slope and secured by earth banks and a retaining wall, and then converted into an Agora, or marketplace. Holy shrines, statues and residential houses stood on each side. The small temple in the middle was probably dedicated to Apollo.

There is a festival site with low grandstands located east of

The atrium houses in ancient Kámiros were luxurious indeed

the Apollo temple. It is likely that rituals to honour this God took place here. To the west, the festival site borders a residential area that lies directly on the main street. It passes by a public bath, a public well (at several sites, preserved earthenware pipes are evidence of ancient water supply and sewage systems) and additional residential quarters, finally ending at the acropolis. Sadly, hardly anything remains from the once stately buildings. From this large area, you can get a good impression of what life was like in a Hellenistic city. *Tues–Fri 8 am–5.40 pm, Sat, Sun 8 am–3 pm; admission 800 Dr; film and video costs an extra 1,000 Dr*

RESTAURANT

New Kamiros
You'll find red barbel, grilled octopus and other delicious seafood, alongside meat dishes, on the menu here. This is a popular destination for residents of Rhodes city, and, at any rate, a good place to recover from your exhausting climb up to old Kámiros. *Tel. 412 41; category 2*

SURROUNDING AREA

Alimniá **(104–105/C–D2)**
★ The presently uninhabited island lures you with a wonderful secluded beach. Fishermen from Chálki bring beach-lovers here for a small fee (£ 3–4 per person when several are travelling together). Today, only a couple of crumbling buildings are located here, among them a monastery dedicated to St George. Fishermen and their families celebrate the name day of the patron saint each year here.

Chálki **(104/A–B2–3)**
This mostly barren, up to 593 m-high, tiny (28 sq km) island off the coast of Rhodes is hardly ever visited by holidaymakers

and remains accordingly unspoilt and quiet. Only about 300 people live on this former sponge-fishing island, almost all of them in the main village of Nimborió. As soon as you enter the harbour, the old houses painted in pastel colours catch your eye. More and more of them are being restored and, in summer, are predominantly rented out as holiday houses to British tourists. Those people from Rhodes who originally came from Chálki also return to the island. Unesco declared Chálki an "Island of Peace and Friendship for the Youth of the World". ✱ Every year in September, young people from around the world come to the island for two weeks of seminars and lectures. You can swim on Póntamos beach, which is not far from Nimborió. The village of Chorió is 3 km from the town. The village was virtually abandoned by its one-time inhabitants and is located at the foot of a fortress ruin dating from the Age of Chivalry. The destination of a full-day hike starting from here is the no-longer inhabited, secluded Ágios Ioánnis Monastery, located in the western part of the island. You can't rent mopeds, let alone cars, on Chálki; if you want to sightsee here, you have to walk and hike.

A boat leaves for Chálki from Kámiros Skála daily at about 2 pm and returns the next morning. There are two connections on Sundays so that one-day excursions can be taken. Twice or three times a week, big car ferries operating between Rhodes and Crete also dock at Chálki.

One place to spend the night at is at the guest house *Kleánthi* (*7 rooms; Tel. 02 41/573 34; no fax; category 3*).

Kámiros Skála **(105/E2)**

This small fishing port south of the ancient city is most interesting for those who want to ferry across to the neighbouring island of Chálki. The locals also appreciate the fish *tavérnas* on the small harbour that are supplied daily with fresh fish. In the rock face behind it, there's an unfinished façade of a stone tomb from the Hellenistic period.

Kritinía Fortress **(105/E2)**

There is a great view of the surrounding area from the Knights of St John fortress. Unfortunately, the fortress has not been made safe, so you should wear sturdy shoes for the climb up and be sure to hold the hands of any small children that may be with you. Coming from Kámiros Skála, turn right on the gravel road shortly before Kritinía (there's a sign). *Always accessible*

KOLÍMBIA

(103/E5) The village lures more and more tourists every year with its wonderful sandy, pebble beaches. Of the 40 hotels built here since 1983, the majority are level complexes that often blend in to the landscape and scenery. Everything here is a smaller version of Faliráki. There are only a few discos, a couple of shops, and a number of *tavérnas*. Surfboards can be rented on the beach and you can reserve tennis courts at large hotels.

RESTAURANT

To Nisáki
The "islet" is a genuine fish *tavérna*. Much of what the owner brings to the table is what he has caught himself from local waters. There's a bar next door and it's only a few steps to the beach. *Not far from Hotel Relax; Tel. 563 60; category 2*

HOTELS

Kolymbia Sky
Because of its quiet location right on the ocean, this hotel is ideal for a relaxing beach holiday. *98 rooms; Tel. 562 71; Fax 562 74; category 2*

Kolymbia Sun
Family-friendly two-storey hotel with pool, about 200 m from the beach. All-inclusive arrangement with rooms big enough for three adults and one child. *65 rooms; Tel. 562 13; Fax 56321; category 2*

SURROUNDING AREA

Ágios Nikólaos Fountouklí **(102/B4–5)**
The Chapel of "St Nicholas of the Hazelnuts" lies in the middle of fields, along the small street that leads from Eleoússa to Profítis Ilías. It dates from the 16th century and was originally the main church of the monastery (from which nothing remains). The monastery was donated by a high-level Byzantine official of Rhodes. The official is depicted, together with his wife, on a fresco next to the west entrance gate. Both are shown presenting the church to Christ, flanked by the Virgin Mary and John the Baptist. On the opposite wall, the couple's three children are depicted. An inscription indicates that the children died virtually simultaneously as a result of an epidemic. The grapevines and birds in the background comfort the parents with the hope that God has taken their children up to the paradise of Heaven. The other depictions follow the traditional Byzantine pattern: saints, prophets and biblical scenes from both the New and Old Testaments. A place to get water is only a few steps away. A table and two long benches shaded by trees invite you to stop and take a break.

Archípolis **(102/C5)**
Up to now, the small, still very "Greek" village on the inland has remained relatively untouched by tourism. There are a couple of simple *tavérnas*, *kafeníons* and private rooms. The Ágios Nekários Monastery, which has been completely repainted with new frescoes, is located along the road to the west coast.

Eptá Pigés **(103/D5)**
It is always comfortably cool under the giant plane trees in the valley of the "Seven Springs". However, it's not a good idea to hike here from Kolímbia in summer, as there isn't any shade along the entire stretch. The attraction of this popular place for outings is a 186-m-long subterranean ditch dating from the

time of the Italian occupation. At the end of the tunnel, there's a pond in the middle of gently waving, green countryside. If you really want to enjoy this idyllic scenery, hike over the hill though which the tunnel leads. Caution: since this is a drinking water conservation area, it's very important to refrain from swimming in the pond! The Seven Springs *tavérna (category 3)*, which serves good plain dishes, such as *souflàki* (meat skewers) and *paidákia* (lamb chops), is located right behind the parking lot. A word of warning: during peak season, it's often very hard to get a table as the restaurant is usually full.

Profítis Ilías **(102/A-B4-5)**
Stags and does, the heraldic animals of the island, still live on the third-highest mountain on Rhodes (798 m). The scenery resembles the Alps – while on Profítis Ilías, you may forget sometimes that it is part of the Aegean island of Rhodes. You can hike or drive up: from Sálakos in the north, Eleoússa in the east or Émbonas in the south-west. There are two hotels located about 100 m below the peak, both originating from the time of the Italian occupation. Unfortunately, both were closed at the time this guide was published.

Tsambíka **(103/E5)**
The uninhabited monastery with its snow-white chapel lies on a mountain between the coastal road and the sea. It is dedicated to the Virgin Mary *(Panagía)*.

The protected bay of Tsambíka offers beautiful sandy beaches

In the dialect of Rhodes, Tsambíka means "glow of the fire", and there's a legend regarding the origin of the monastery that everyone tells just a little bit differently. One version maintains that a childless married couple had almost given up hope of having children. One night, a man saw the mysterious glow of a fire on the mountain. The next night, he saw it again, and once again on the following night. He hiked up and found an icon of the Virgin Mary at the location where he had seen the fire. He solemnly promised to build a monastery for her if his wife became pregnant. When he arrived home, his wife informed him that they were expecting a child. They had a girl, who they named Tsambíka, "glow of fire", and the man built the monastery as promised. Today, Tsambíka and Tsambíkos are still common first names on Rhodes.

The monastery chapel is still a place of pilgrimage, especially for young women hoping for a happy marriage and children. Most of the way is concrete so you can drive up with a car or moped, although most of the pilgrims walk as much of the way as possible. The pilgrimage is supposed to be especially successful if you carry a sack with heavy stones on your shoulder for the last leg of the pilgrimage (at least 20 minutes long).

The Tsambíka restaurant is located on a small plateau before you begin the last leg of the climb. As the sign announces, locals are welcome to celebrate weddings and baptisms there – and holidaymakers can exchange Drachmas in case they didn't bring along enough to get a bite to eat.

A white gate leads the way into the monastery. To the left, there's an empty room where pilgrims can sleep. In the small room on the right, you can sign the thick guest book. Many local visitors have immortalized themselves with lengthy, touching letters to "Dearest Virgin Mary".

Before you begin the ascent, you can enjoy the view of the bays of the east coast and above all, the sandy beach of Tsambíka, one of the most beautiful beaches on the whole island.

For security reasons, the miracle-working icon of the Virgin Mary is no longer housed in the unsupervised mountain chapel. It has been bequeathed to Káto Tsambíka Monastery, which lies directly along the main road to Líndos, about 1 km from the turn-off to the mountain peak chapel. The monastery church dates from the 18th century and houses the precious iconostasis. Glistening Venetain chandeliers hang down from the ceilings.

On 7/8 September, the birthday of the Virgin Mary, many people, especially pilgrims, make their way to the chapel, which hosts the holy icon on those two days. The footpath from the restaurant to the peak is illuminated on these two days.

Island beauty with many faces

These routes are marked in green on the map on the inside front cover and in the Road Atlas beginning on page 102

① TRACES OF ANCIENT GREECE AND THE AGE OF CHIVALRY

Crash course in history: today, you'll get to know all four Rhodes cities of Ancient Greece as well as all the important fortresses built by the Knights of St John. You'll pass by the ocean several times so that you can take swimming breaks. You should start early in order to take full advantage of the opening hours of the archaeological sites. Monday is not a good day to take this tour because some places are closed then. The length of the round-trip tour from Rhodes and back is about 210 km and takes between eight and ten hours.

The first stop on the tour is *Monte Smith (p. 43)*. The *acropolis of Rhodes* stood on this mountain in Ancient times. Italian archaeologists have reconstructed the stadium and theatre, but only three and a half columns are still standing.

From the Monte Smith, drive to the divided highway which connects Rhodes with Líndos. Continue past *Faliráki (p. 82)*, with its tall hotels, Rhodes becomes more rural.

After you pass *Kolímbia (p. 87)*, you can see the *Tsambíka Monastery (p. 89)* on the left, high up on a mountain. After passing the turn-off to the completely unspoilt, dream-like sandy *Tsambíka Beach*, the road begins an ascent. The *Valley Monastery of Tsambíka (p. 90)*, with its beautiful church and rustic pub is located around a left-hand bend.

The next sightseeing stop is in *Archángelos (p. 79)*, the second-largest city on the island. A short walk leads to the *ruins of the knights' fortress.* After this, you should have a seat in the old café at the bus stop and watch the goings-on of the village.

After Archángelos, the divided highway ascends the next hill, and then descends again to the largest *orange orchard* on Rhodes, which surrounds the village of *Malónas (p. 81).* The village of *Charáki (p. 81),* with the *Féraklos fortress (p. 82),* is located here on the coast. At the foot of the fortress hill, *the ruins of a medieval sugar refinery* are located about

200 m behind the last houses of the site, on the open field. Cane sugar was an important economic factor for the Order of the Knights of St John of Jerusalem. The ruins are fenced-off, but you can easily see from the outside.

The first view of *Líndos (p. 57)* inspires every tourist to put on their brakes for the first time on the tour. The stately *acropolis* towers above the white houses of this unique village. Ancient Greeks crowned the acropolis rock with a temple; the Knights built a castle there.

After a stroll through the village, drive further along the west coast until you reach *Gennádi (p. 65).* Here, you turn off towards the inland and reach *Istrios* via *Váti.* From here, you can drive to *Apolakkiá (p. 75)* and, after about 5 km, on the right, you'll see two large apses that were part of a five-naved basilica from early Christian times.

After Apolakkiá, the next site is *Monólithos (p. 77),* located very close to the eponymous photogenic castle high on a hill above the sea. Along the way, you should take a short break in *Siánna (p. 78)* and eat some yoghurt with honey before continuing along the west coast. After passing *Kritinía (p. 87)*, a very steep road turns off to the fortress. If you've seen enough fortresses by now, continue on until you reach the tiny fishing port of *Kámiros Skála (p. 87)* and then on to the *excavations of the ancient city of Kámiros.* There's still another destination left on the tour, shortly before the city of Rhodes: the plateau of *Filérimos (p. 52),* with it's ancient ruins and medieval monastery.

② SMALL CHURCHES, QUIET VILLAGES

If you're searching for the authentic Greece, you'll have more luck finding it in the inland villages of the island than you will in the coastal towns. This tour takes you to many small villages as well as to a number of small Byzantine churches and monasteries. Some are kept closed to prevent theft of icons, others are open to the public. They do not only offer aesthetic enjoyment, but also fascinate with their scenic locations. A jeep is not absolutely necessary for this tour, but it does make the shortcuts via gravel roads and bumpy streets more manageable. The length of the return trip from Faliráki and back is 250 km. Duration is at least eight to ten hours.

You pass *Faliráki (p. 82)* on the divided highway, but turn off after only 5 km into the village of *Afántou (p. 72)*, and from there take the street into the big inland village of *Psínthos (p. 75)*, with its lively village square. A small street continues on to *Archípolis (p. 88)*, a village that has remained especially rural. The *Agía Triáda chapel (p. 74)*, with frescoes from the 15th and 16th centuries, is located about 2,300 m to the left of Psínthos.

From Archípolis, take a short detour via the road to *Kolímbia.* After about 2 km, you'll see the *Ágios Nektários Church.* A massive hollow plane tree stands in front of the entrance to the church. On the opposite side of the street, the local government is beginning construction of a woodlands park.

From Archípolis, your tour continues to *Eleoússa (pp. 88, 89)* and on to the *Ágios Nikólaos*

Fountoukli Church (p. 88), an extremely beautiful sacred building. After viewing the interior rooms, return to Eleoússa and from there, drive through the very peaceful villages of *Platánia* and *Apóllonas* to *Émbonas (p. 76)*, where you can visit a wine cellar and eat lunch if you'd like.

The next sightseeing destination is located in the south: the *Skiádi Monastery (p. 79)*, which houses a miracle-working icon of the Virgin Mary. From there, you'll drive on what is currently a very rough, bumpy patch over the mountain to Mesanagrós. It's best to ask in the monastery about the current status of the road – it's likely that you'll have to take a detour via *Kattaviá (p. 76)* to get to nearby *Mesanagrós (p. 76)*. If you go to this village, you are rewarded with a must-see church. The owner of the neighbouring village café keeps the key to the church, and you can eat some good plain cooking in the café as well.

Back on the road from Mesanagrós to Lachaniá it's worthwhile to take a detour to the *Pilgrimage Church of Ágios Thomás (p. 77)*. *Lachaniá* reveals all its rural charm, especially if you park your vehicle on the main road and go down into the *Taverne Plátanos*. From Lachaniá, continue north. *Two highlights of this day trip* are still to be experienced: a quick side trip to the mountain village of *Asklipión (p. 64)* with its fresco-adorned church and a small museum. The other side trip takes you to *Thári Monastery (p. 67)* near *Láerma (p. 66)*. After a long interim, monks are once again living in this monastery.

If there's still enough time and you're still up for more sight-seeing, drive through a fragrant pine forest from *Lárdos (p. 67)* to the *Ipsenís Convent (p. 65)*, where hospitable nuns live. You can drive back to Faliráki along the well-paved east coast road.

③ AN ABUNDANCE OF NATURE AND BEAUTIFUL BEACHES

This day trip is not about historical places of interest. The pleasures of nature and swimming are the focus of this tour – a convertible would be the best for this trip, of course. You can take this tour as a complete island round trip and return to your holiday location along the west coast. However, the fastest route from the southern part of the island back to your holiday domicile is by way of the well-paved east coast road. The length of the tour to and from Rhodes city is 200 km, and takes at least seven to nine hours.

The prelude to the pretty beaches along the east coast is the small *Bay of Ladikó (p. 85)*, seen shortly after *Faliráki (p. 82)*. There's only one *tavérna* on the short, but rarely full sandy beach. A dusty but driveable road leads you to *Anthony Quinn Bay (p. 84)*.

Kolímbia (p. 87) has *two nice sandy beaches*. The northern one is several kilometres long, but is visually a little less appealing because of the flat hinterland. In contrast, the southern beach is bordered by a low but steep coastline of bizarre rock formations, making it very appealing to the eye. Coming from Kolímbia, if you don't continue driving directly south, but instead take a detour to *Eptá Pigés (p. 88)*, located in the interior, you'll come to a subterranean ditch, and after going over the hill, you'll find a pond in the middle of the gently rolling, green countryside. Try to resist the temptation to go swimming: it's a reservoir for drinking water!

Only 2 km south of Kolímbia, a steep road turns off to the *Tsambíka Beach (p. 89)*, one of the nicest the island has to offer. It's almost 1 km long and completely unspoilt. There is only one *tavérna* and several makeshift snack bars here. Otherwise, it is still completely in its natural state. Especially nice: the wind has blown the sand to the slopes on the southern part of the beach, making it appear that you are lying in front of huge dunes.

Time for lunch? In *Charáki (p. 81)* you can eat excellent fish in the Argo restaurant. If you prefer to visit another sandy beach, you can hike or drive north of Charáki to *Agáthi bay*, viewed as an insider tip by Rhodes experts because it's not very crowded.

In contrast, both of the pretty *sandy beaches of Líndos (p. 57)* are very crowded. Visit them another time and drive past Líndos to *Péfki (p. 68)*. Along the way, there is a nice view of *Ágios Pávlos Bay (p. 58)*, where the Apostle Paul allegedly went ashore.

At *Lárdos (p. 67)*, another divided highway begins. You'll see yet another small *sandy bay* on the left after driving only a few hundred metres. The longest east coast beach begins shortly after *Kiotári (p. 66)*. This wide stretch of partly sandy, partly pebble beach spans far beyond *Gennádi (p. 65)*.

The southernmost hamlet on the east coast is *Plimmíri (p. 67)*, with its empty *sandy beach* and a nice *tavérna Zoodóchos Pigé* next door to the scenic church. It's built on the foundation of an early Christian basilica from the fifth/sixth century. Beautiful marble slabs and columns from the basilica were used to build the present-day church.

The island village that is the furtherest away from the city of Rhodes is *Kattaviá (p. 76)*. Several *tavérnas* on the village square invite you to sit and take a break, but you can also eat on *the beach of Prassoníssi (p. 78)*, located on the southern point of the island. This beach would certainly be the nicest one on the island if it weren't for the clumps of tar and other flotsam and jetsam that wash up on the shore.

If you don't want to take the faster route along the east coast for the return trip to the northern part of the island, you'll reach the western shores of the island shortly after Kattaviá. You won't find any more pretty beaches in this area, but the *mountainous countryside* is a nice change of place. If you still have a lot of time on the way back, you might like to take a little side trip to *Butterfly Valley (p. 74)*. From there, you can return to Faliráki or to another holiday resort by way of the village of *Psínthos (p. 75)*.

Practical information

Important addresses and useful information for your visit on Rhodes

ADMISSION

Visitors under the age of 18 are admitted free to those museums and archaeological sites that are state-run. Seniors over 65 receive discounts.

AMERICAN & BRITISH ENGLISH

Marco Polo travel guides are written in British English. In North America certain terms and usages deviate from British usage. Some of the more frequently encountered examples are (American given first):
baggage = luggage; cab = taxi; car rental = car hire; drugstore = chemist; fall = autumn; first floor = ground floor; freeway/highway = motorway; gas(oline) = petrol; railroad = railway; restroom = toilet/lavatory; streetcar = tram; subway = underground/tube; toll-free numbers = freephone numbers; trailer = caravan; trunk = boot (of a car); vacation = holiday; wait staff = waiter/waitress; zip code = post code.

BANKS/CURRENCY

Banks and post offices change currency and cash travel cheques. Banks also cash Eurocheques (up to 50,000 Dr). Opening hours: *Banks Mon–Thurs 8 am–2 pm, Fri 8 am–1.30 pm, Post Offices Mon–Fri 7.30 am–3 pm, longer in large tourist areas.* Withdrawals from post office savings accounts cannot be made! At some banks, you can use your EC card/bank card and PIN number to withdraw cash from a cash machine.

CAMPING

Camping is permitted only in designated camping areas. The only one on the island is *Camping Faliráki; Tel. 853 58; Fax 855 16.*

CUSTOMS

The following goods may be imported into Greece by visitors without incurring customs duty by: (a) Residents of European countries with goods bought duty-free outside the EU: 200 cigarettes or 50 cigars or 100 cigarillos or 250 g of tobacco; 1 litre of alcoholic beverage over 22% or 2 litres of wine; 50 g of perfume and 250 ml of eau de cologne; gifts up to a total value of 25,000 Dr. (b) Residents of countries outside Europe with goods obtained duty-free outside the EU: 400 cigarettes or 100 cigars or 200 cigarillos or 500 g of tobacco; limits for other goods same as for (a) above.

DISABLED PEOPLE

Due to a lack of special facilities, Rhodes is not an ideal destination for physically handicapped people.

DRIVING

A national driver's licence is sufficient. It is recommended to bring your international insurance card. Gas stations are frequent and unleaded gas is sold everywhere. In Greece, all cars require premium gas. Breakdown service provided on the island and throughout the country by ELPA, the Greek automobile association: *Tel. 104.*

On Rhodes it's compulsory to wear seatbelts. Maximum speed in residential zones and the city is 50 km/h; on country roads 90 km/h. Honking before reaching a blind corner is the norm, however it is prohibited in residential and city areas. The alcohol limit is 0.5 – severe sentences for drunk driving!

Rental cars can be rented at all holiday resorts and at the airport. Comprehensive insurance does not cover damage to tyres or to the underside of the car.

EMBASSIES

British Embassy
Odós Ploutarchou 1, 106 75 Athens; Tel. 1/723 6211; Fax 1/727 2734; britania@hol.gr

Letters and transcription

How are Greek words transcribed into Roman letters? Up to now, a uniform system has not prevailed. In this text in this travel guide, words are written in the way that comes closest to their pronunciation. On the maps, however, a new transcription system is used that has been declared as internationally binding. Where necessary, we have added the map version to the text (in parentheses). The most frequent differences: "y" on the map is "i"in the text, "ou" is "u" and "ei" is "i". We use the English name for some places, for example "Athens" instead of "Athinai" and "Patros" instead of "Patrai". The following table displays the letters of the Greek alphabet and their Roman equivalents.

The Greek Alphabet and Transcription

Α	α	a	Η	η	i	Ν	ν	n	Τ	τ	t
Β	β	v, w	Θ	ϑ	th	Ξ	ξ	ks, x	Υ	υ	i, y
Γ	γ	g, i	Ι	ι	i, j	Ο	ο	o	Φ	φ	f
Δ	δ	d	Κ	κ	k	Π	π	p	Χ	χ	ch
Ε	ε	e	Λ	λ	l	Ρ	ρ	r	Ψ	ψ	ps
Ζ	ζ	s, z	Μ	μ	m	Σ	σ, ς	s, ss	Ω	ώ	o

United States Embassy
Leoforos Vassilissis Sophias 91, 101 60 Athens; Tel. 1/721 2 9 51; Fax 1/645 6 2 82; usembassy@usisathens.gr

Canadian Embassy
Odós Ioannou Gennadiou 4, 11521 Athens; Tel. 1/727 34 00; Fax 1/727 34 60; athns@dfait-maeci.gc.ca

EMERGENCIES

Police: *100*
Tourist Police Rhodes City: *23 3 29 or 27 4 23 (corner of Odós Papágou and Odós Makaríou)*

HEALTH

General Hospital
(Jenikó Nossokomío), Rhodes city, Odós Erythroú Stavroú, Emergency Room Tel. 255 55

Pharmacies *(farmakíon)* are officially closed Sat and Sun. A list of pharmacies that are open for emergencies hangs in pharmacy windows and is also listed in the free English papers. Securing travel health insurance before leaving home is highly recomended.

INFORMATION

Greek/Hellenic National Tourism Organisation (GNTO)
4 Conduit Street, London W11 3TP; Tel. 020/77345 99 7; Fax 020/72 871 36 9; e-mail: eot-greek-touristoffice@binternet.com

1300 Bay Street, Toronto, Ontario, M5R 3K8; Tel. 416/968 22 20; Fax 416/9686 53 3; e-mail: grnto.tor @sympatico.ca

Embassy of Greece (Hellas)
2221 Massachusetts Avenue NW, Washington, DC, 20008; Tel. 202/ 939 58 00; Fax 202/939 58 24; greece@greekembassy.org

INTERNET

Information about Rhodes can be found at: *www.travel-greece.com*
For updated ferry connections, go to *www.gtpnet.com*

MEASURES & WEIGHTS

1 cm	0.39 inches
1 m	1.09 yards (3.28 feet)
1 km	0.62 miles
1 m²	1.20 sq. yards
1 ha	2.47 acres
1 km²	0.39 sq. miles
1 g	0.035 ounces
1 kg	2.21 pounds
1 British ton	1016 kg
1 US ton	907 kg

1 litre is equivalent to 0.22 Imperial gallons and 0.26 US gallons

NEWSPAPERS

Foreign daily newspapers and magazines – for the most part with a one-day delay – can be found everywhere on the island. The English daily newspaper *Athens News* is published in Greece itself.

OPENING HOURS

Most shops on the island are open from Monday to Friday 9 am–1.30 pm and 4 pm–6 pm. During the tourist season, they are usually open late in the evening and on weekends as well. They are often closed on Monday and Wednesday afternoons. There is at least one small shop *(bakáliko)* in every village. Most are closed between 2 pm and 5 pm.

PASSPORT & VISA

Citizens of Great Britain, Canada and the USA need a valid passport. A visa is not required. Travellers coming from USA and Canada must have a return ticket.

PETS

Regulations for bringing pets into Greece require an international vaccination card or a public veterinarian health certificate that is not older than 14 days.

POST & TELEPHONE

Post offices are usually open Mon–Fri 7.30 am–3 pm. The main post office in Rhodes city *(Platía Dimarchíou/ Mandráki)* is open Mon–Fri 7.30 am–8 pm. You can also buy stamps at many kiosks and hotel reception desks, as well as in many souvenir shops.

Public card phones are located in most areas. Telephone cards with 100 units (1,000 Dr) can be purchased at all kiosks and in many supermarkets. Telephone cards with 500 units (4,200 Dr) can be purchased at the offices of the telephone company (OTE). It's better to avoid making phone calls from hotels and travel agencies because the rates are usually very steep indeed. Economy rate times for a long-distance call: 10 pm–8 am. Mobile phones are widespread, the range is good.
Country code for USA/Canada: 001
Country code for the UK: 0044
Country code for Greece: 00 30
The three different area codes for Rhodes:
In Rhodes City, Afántou, Soroní: 02 41
The western parts of the island (e.g. Apolakkiá, Monólithos, Émbonas): 02 46
The eastern parts of the island (e.g. Archángelos, Líndos, Lárdos, Kattaviá): 02 44

PUBLIC TOILETS

With the exception of very good hotels and restaurants, toilet paper is not allowed to be thrown into the toilet bowl; instead, use the wastepaper basket.

PUBLIC TRANSPORT

Long-Distance Coaches

The bus company KTEL goes to the eastern coast, RODA to the west coast. In the city of Rhodes, the main terminals are located at the *New Market (Néa Agor)*, KTEL in front of the *tourist association*, RODA, on *Odós Papágou* at the entrance to "Sound and Light". Busses start departing in the early morning in intervals of between 30 minutes and three hours. Fares are paid on board and cost between 430 Dr and 1,900 Dr.

Municipalbusses in Rhodes city

Five bus lines depart from the *Platía Eleftherías (Néa Agor/Mandráki)* bus terminal. Tickets can be purchased in advance at the RODA counter (Mandráki) or at the kiosk (approx. 210 Dr).

RADIO/TV

Private foreign language channels can be received in hotels and guesthouses that have satellite dishes.

TAXIS

The grey or blue taxis queue up at the airport, in front of the large hotels and at the taxi rank in Rhodes city (Mandráki). To order a taxi by telephone, ring: *64734* or *64712*. The starting rate is about 379 Dr, every additional kilometre costs 128 Dr; rates are doubled outside the locality and after midnight. Luggage costs extra.

TIME

The time is one hour later than Central Europe.

TIPPING

It's customary to leave about a 5–10% tip.

WHEN TO GO

Except for the rainy and stormy season from December until mid-March, it's always a good time to visit Rhodes.

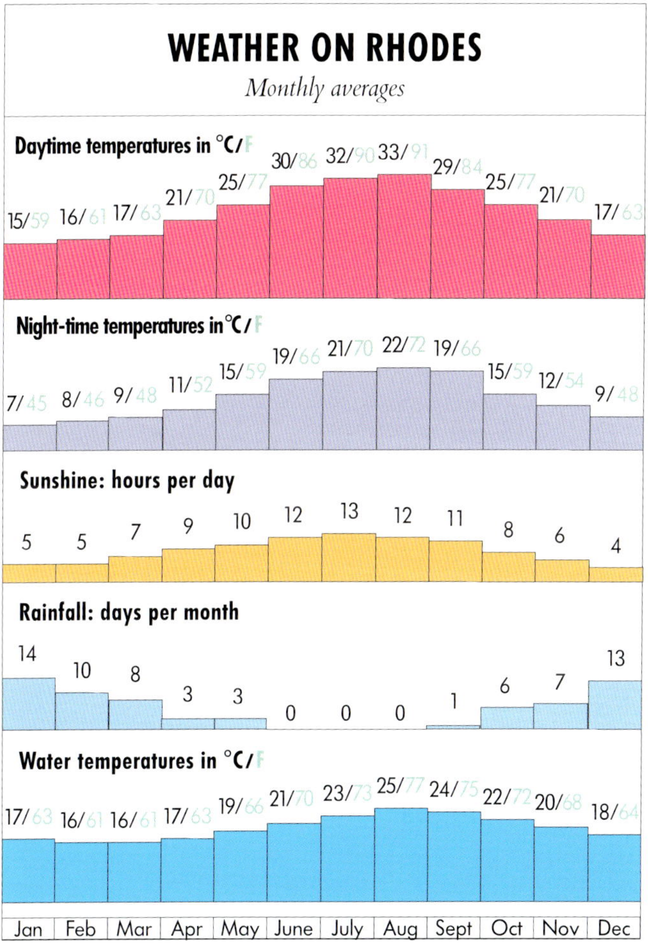

Do's and don'ts

How to avoid some of the traps and pitfalls that may face the unwary traveller

Wildly taking pictures

Most residents of Rhodes like to have a picture taken. However, they don't like photographers who act like hunters. Before you press the shutter release, you should politely ask for the subject's consent with a smile.

Do enjoy driving without remorse

You can certainly get to know Rhodes better if you have your own vehicle. In many villages, busses are very infrequent and are often overflowing with people. For this reason, car and motorcycle rental agencies all over Rhodes tempt you with special offers. Before you jump on one, a couple of hints: Don't overestimate yourself! Many tourists rent a moped or car that they can't safely keep under control, or they step on the accelerator harder than they would do at home. Such drives often end in the hospital – or worse. Remember that you're not used to the vehicle, streets or the weather. A bicycle is certainly sufficient for short stretches!

Motorcycle drivers should bring their own helmet with them. Many rental agencies have either unsafe helmets or none at all (although a helmet is mandatory in Greece, even for moped drivers!).

Partial insurance coverage is automatically included in the contract (non-liability towards third parties). Many rental agencies offer comprehensive insurance in addition. Take a look at the conditions and fine print before you sign anything.

Visiting churches in your bathing suit

On Rhodes, many are happy when people visit churches or participate in church services. Unfortunately, more and more tourists stroll through monasteries wearing shorts or their bathing suits or obtrusively take photographs during religious pilgrimages. If you can't respect the religious feelings of others, it's better to avoid visiting churches.

Assuming everything's a rip-off

Nobody is perfect. Among the mostly honest people of Rhodes, there are a few who want to take advantage of tourists. Sometimes, however, the customer is wrong. A cover charge always has to be paid along with your meal (60–300 Dr). After fare increases, for financial reasons, bus and ferry tickets showing the old price are used up before the new ones are put into circulation.

Road Atlas of Rhodes

Please refer to back cover for an overview of this Road Atlas

A
B
C
1
2
3
4
5
6
Piräefs 16h
Kos 4h
Symi 1h
MEDITERRANEAN
SEA
Chalkī 2h
Karpathos 5h
Akra Mīnas
Kameiros
Kalavarda
Monī Sotirōs
Fanai
198
Sorōnī
Kato
Kalamōn
Theologos
Monī Sylla
Argiros
Plati
Psinthos
480
277
411
15
27
698
Salakos
(210)
Kapi
Dimylia
Elafos-Elafina
798
Profitis Ilias
Nanoi
Ag Nikolaos
Fountoukli
641
Platania
Eleousa
Ag.Eleousa
Archip
Apollōna
(310)
Monī Kariōna
28
551
Messov
12
Embonas
Εμπωνας
367
Assouri
16
avyros
1215
MoniArtamyti
397
Platanero
Mákkaris
Malōn
Monī Kamirou
324
Monī Ag.Isidoros
360
Masarī
218
Gaidou
107
102

D
E
F
1
2
3
4
5
6
Marmaris 3h
Megisti
Lemesos 20 h, Hefa 40h
RODOS
ΡΟΔΟΣ
Akra Zōnari
Enydreio
ELPA
Palati Ippotōn
Monte Smith
110
KRĪTIKA
Ormos Trianta
IALYSSOS
(TRIANTA)
ΙΑΛΥΣΣΟΣ
IXIA
KANDILI
Rodini Parko
TREIS
Kremastī
Κρεμαστη
Panagia Kremastī
Ag.Ioannis
Paradisi
Παραδεισι
Paradeisiou
Filerimos
267
Ialyssos
Sgourou
(Asgourou)
Kallithea
Akra Vōdi
Pastida
Damatria
Koskinou
Κοσκινου
Thermes Kallitheas
Maritsa
Μαριτσα
416
263
Ormos Kallitheas
Kalamōn
Koumouli
Monī Eleousas
Faliraki
Kalythiai
Καλυθιαι
Kalopetras
25
Monī Amos
Akra Ladiko
Psinthos
330
Psalidī
362
Alogna
Ag.Triada
Afantou
Αφαντου
Panagia Parmeniōtissis
Ormos Afantou
Katholikī Afantou
Ag. Nektários
Loutánī
456
Kolymbia
Akra Vagia
Epta Piges
Seven Springs
341
Monī Tsambikas
Ormos Archangelos
Petrona
(180)
Archangelos
Αρχαγγελος
Stegna
Profitis Ilias
512
18
Akra Archangelos
Ormos Malōnos
Lindos
Ag.Agathī
Faraklos
Charakion
5 km

A
B
C
1
2
3
4
5
6
Alimia
Αλιμιά
262
Agios Theodōros
Chalkī
Χαλκη
Akra Limanari
Kefalos
Maistros
593
Profitis Ilias
578
Chalkī
Ag.Iōannis
3
Chorion
268
Nisaki
Krevatia
Akra Myrtos
Akra Ikalos
Akra Armenistīs
319
Armenistis
MEDITERRANEAN
Akra Monolithos
Strongilo I.
SEA
Diafanion 2h
5 km

D
E
F
Akra Mīnas
Kam
Rodos 2h
15
27
Mandrikon
Akra Katsouni
Akra Kopria
Skala Kāmiros
Kapi
Nanoi
Kastellos Krītinia
Makry I.
Krītinia
Mon
12
Strongilī
Monī Amartou
Amartos
Embonas
Εμπωνας
agoussa
Atavyros
1215
3
MonīArtamyti
Akra Glifada
Lakkion
Monī Ag.Isidoros
1062
Agios Isidōros
Akramitīs
825
Siana
(450)
4
548
585
Monolithos
(280)
41
astellos
(240)
Monī Tha
402
Ag. Georgios o Vardas
Istrios
Profilia
Kourkoutachi
Akra Fournoi
5
496
Strongilī
Ormos Apolakkias
Ag.Eirinī
Apolakkia
Agios Nikolaos
Arnitha
Vati
Kīmissi tis Theotōkou
513
6
Koukouliāri
105
106
341
Gennadi
563

A
B
C
105
106
1
2
3
4
5
6
Akra Glifada
Lakkion
Atavyros
1062
Agios Isidōros
Moni
319
Armenistis
Akramitis
825
Siana
(450)
548
585
41
Kastellos
(240)
Monolithos
(280)
Akra Monolithos
Strongilo I.
Akra Fournoi
Ormos
Apolakkias
Ag. Georgios o Vardas
Istrios
Koukoutachi
Profilia
496
Strongili
402
Ag.Eirini
Apolakkia
Agios Nikolaos
Arnitha
Vati
513
Koukouliari
Moni Skiadi
563
Mesanagros
386
Kimissi tis Theotōkou
Ag.Thomas
Chtenies
306
319
Lachania
20
Kattavia
Agios Pavlos
Chochlakas
236
189
Karávolas
Plimmiri
Akra Viglas
Vrulia
Oros
Akra Prasonisi
Prasonisi

D
E
F
102
Monī Kamirou
Masarī
Ag.Agathi
Charaki
Ag.Isidoros
360
218
Gaidouropotamos
Ag Geōrgios Lorima
Laerma
(400)
220
Monī Tharī
363
389
Inko
371
Kalathos
Ormos
Vlicha
Akra Ag.
Aimilianos
Vlicha
Pilon
Lardos
Monī Ipsenis
Lindos
Λινδος
458
Marmári
Akropolī tīs Lindou
Lim.Apost. Pavlou
Pentanīsos
Kontari
Asklīpieion
309
Ormos Lardos
Pefkoi
Pefkos
Vrachi
Akra Lardos
(Fōkas)
Kimissi tis Theotōkou
Monī tīs Metamorfōseōs
Tsambikas
Paralia
Kiotari
Gennadi
Ormos
Gennadiou
MEDITERRANEAN
SEA
g.Geōrgiou
ra Istros
5 km
1
2
3
4
5
6

A
B
C
1
2
3
4
5
6
Patmos 6h
Antimacheia
Pylion
843
Kardamaina
Skala
Kefalos
Ag. Stefanos
428
Latra
Akra Krikelos
Kos
Κως
Kos 1½h
Kos 3h
Bodrum 2h
Reşadıy
Körmen
İnce Burun
Karaköy
Boz Dağı
1144
Döşeme
Kargi
Mesudiye
İskandil Burnu
Knidos
Yazıköy
Dereboynu Burnu
182
Gyali
3/4h
Mandrakion
Paloi
698
Emporeios
Kratir
Nikia
Pergousa
Piräefs 16h
Nisyros
Νισυρος
4h
1½h
1h
Kandelioussa
Notioi (Dodekanisou) Sporades
Akra Orfos
Ag. Antonios
Megalon Chōrion
651
Tilos
Τηλος
Livadia
Akra Trachilos
Antitilos
Chalkī
Χάλκη
593
Chalk
Akra Myrtos
Arme
Iraklion 10h
Karpathion Pelagos
2h
Stenon Karpathou
Akra Paraspori
Saria
Σαρια
Astakida
Diafanion
Olympos
718
Karpathos
Καρπαθος
Karpathos 1¼h
Karpathos 5h
Spoa
Messochōrion
1215
Kali Limni

D
E
F
Yarımadası
Yuvacık
Marmaris Denizi
Mağarası
Marmaris
Günlüce
Adaköy
İçmeler
Karaağaç Körfezi
Yılancık Adası
Aktur
Emecik
Erine
Hisarönü
Reşadiye
Datça Körfezi
Datça
TÜRKİYE
Kastabos
Turgut
Hydas
Turunç
Marmaris Limanı
Çiftlik
Kadırga Burnu
Hisarönü Körfezi
Selimiye
Bayır
Bozburun
Bozburun Yarımadası
Nimos
Söğüt
Sömbeki Körfezi
Taşlıca
Emporeios
Symi
Pedion
Kasareia
Symi
Συμη
Moni Ag. Panormitis
Loryma
Kara Burun
Sesklion
Akra Zōnari
Ialyssos
RODOS
ΡΟΔΟΣ
Kremasti
Rodos (Diagoras)
(Trianta)
Ialyssos
Paradisi
Megisti
Lemesos 20h
Hefa 40h
Koskinou
Thermes Kallithea
Sorōni
Epanō
Maritsa
Kalamōn
M.Eleousas
Faliraki
Kalavarda
Kalythiai
Kameiros
Psinthos
Afantou
Alimia
Mandrikon
Salakos
Eleousa
Kamirou Skala
Apollona
Archipolis
Kolymbia
Kastellos
Kritinia
Moni Tsambikas
Embōnas
Attavyros
Moni Artamyti
Malōn
Archangelos
Moni Kamiroa
Faraklos
Siana
Ag. Isidōros
Laerma
Charakion
Rodos
Ροδος
Monolithos
Moni Thari
Kalathos
Istrios
Lardos
Lindos
Apolakkia
Asklipieion
Pefkoi
Arnitha
Vation
Akra Lardos
Gennadion
Mesanagros
Lachania
Kattavia
Chochlakas
Akra Prasonīsion
MEDITERRANEAN
SEA
10km
1
2
3
4
5
6

ROAD ATLAS LEGEND

Legende	Beispiel	Legend
Autobahn · Gebührenpflichtige Anschlussstelle · Gebührenstelle · Anschlussstelle mit Nummer · Rasthaus mit Übernachtung · Raststätte · Erfrischungsstelle · Tankstelle · Parkplatz mit und ohne WC	Trento 11	Motorway · Toll junction · Toll station · Junction with number · Motel · Restaurant · Snackbar · Filling-station · Parking place with and without WC
Autobahn in Bau und geplant mit Datum der Verkehrsübergabe	Datum Date	Motorway under construction and projected with completion date
Zweibahnige Straße (4-spurig)		Dual carriageway (4 lanes)
Fernverkehrsstraße · Straßennummern	14 E45	Trunk road · Road numbers
Wichtige Hauptstraße		Important main road
Hauptstraße · Tunnel · Brücke		Main road · Tunnel · Bridge
Nebenstraßen		Minor roads
Fahrweg · Fußweg		Track · Footpath
Wanderweg (Auswahl)		Tourist footpath (selection)
Eisenbahn mit Fernverkehr		Main line railway
Zahnradbahn, Standseilbahn		Rack-railway, funicular
Kabinenschwebebahn · Sessellift		Aerial cableway · Chair-lift
Autofähre		Car ferry
Personenfähre		Passenger ferry
Schifffahrtslinie		Shipping route
Naturschutzgebiet · Sperrgebiet		Nature reserve · Prohibited area
Nationalpark, Naturpark · Wald		National park, natural park · Forest
Straße für Kfz. gesperrt		Road closed to motor vehicles
Straße mit Gebühr		Toll road
Straße mit Wintersperre	XII-II	Road closed in winter
Straße für Wohnanhänger gesperrt bzw. nicht empfehlenswert		Road closed or not recommended for caravans
Touristenstraße · Pass	Weinstraße 1510	Tourist route · Pass
Schöner Ausblick · Rundblick · Landschaftlich bes. schöne Strecke		Scenic view · Panoramic view · Route with beautiful scenery

Golfplatz · Schwimmbad	Golf-course · Swimming pool
Ferienzeltplatz · Zeltplatz	Holiday camp · Transit camp
Jugendherberge · Sprungschanze	Youth hostel · Ski jump
Kirche im Ort, freistehend · Kapelle	Church · Chapel
Kloster · Klosterruine	Monastery · Monastery ruin
Schloss, Burg · Schloss-, Burgruine	Palace, castle · Ruin
Turm · Funk-, Fernsehturm	Tower · Radio-, TV-tower
Leuchtturm · Kraftwerk	Lighthouse · Power station
Wasserfall · Schleuse	Waterfall · Lock
Bauwerk · Marktplatz, Areal	Important building · Market place, area
Ausgrabungs- u. Ruinenstätte · Feldkreuz	Arch. excavation, ruins · Calvary
Dolmen · Menhir	Dolmen · Menhir
Hünen-, Hügelgrab · Soldatenfriedhof	Cairn · Military cemetery
Hotel, Gasthaus, Berghütte · Höhle	Hotel, inn, refuge · Cave

Kultur	Beispiel	Culture
Malerisches Ortsbild · Ortshöhe	WIEN (171)	Picturesque town · Elevation
Eine Reise wert	★★ MILANO	Worth a journey
Lohnt einen Umweg	★ TEMPLIN	Worth a detour
Sehenswert	Andermatt	Worth seeing
Landschaft		**Landscape**
Eine Reise wert	★★ Las Cañadas	Worth a journey
Lohnt einen Umweg	★ Texel	Worth a detour
Sehenswert	Dikti	Worth seeing

This index lists all the main places and sights and important persons mentioned in this guide. Numbers in bold indicate a main entry, italics a photograph

What do you get for your money?

At the time of publication, one British Pound had a value of about 563 Dr. What you get for it depends on where you go. In modest cafés, you'll pay about 300 Dr for a cup of Nescafé (instant coffee); in fancier cafés and hotels, however, it can cost up to 800 Dr. Likewise, for half a litre of draught beer, one proprietor charges 500 Dr while another one takes 1,400 Dr. A double room with a bathroom costs from 9,000 Dr; luxury hotels charge up to 45,100 Dr.

To rent a surfboard, you'll pay 3,400 Dr and up, and the rental fee for a bike is at least 2,250 Dr per day; discounts are granted for weekly rentals. Rental fees for a motorcycle (50 cubic, e.g. Yamaha Chappy) are 5,650 Dr and up per day; runabouts (e.g. Fiat Panda) from local companies, incl. partial insurance coverage and taxes, are approx. 11,300 Dr per day. Mopeds per day run to approx. 5,650. Gas is about 260 Dr per litre. The taxi ride from the city of Rhodes to Koskinoú (8 km) costs about 1,450 Dr, 1 km with the municipalbus costs about 240 Dr.

Credit cards and cheques are often not accepted in small villages. Exception: large souvenir shops and textile shops, major hotels and rental car places (Eurocard/Mastercard and Visa are the main cards accepted).

Dr	£	US$	Can$
100	0.18	0.25	0.37
250	0.44	0.63	0.93
500	0.89	1.25	1.86
750	1.33	1.88	2.79
1000	1.78	2.50	3.72
1500	2.66	3.76	5.57
2000	3.55	5.01	7.43
3000	5.33	7.51	11.15
4000	7.10	10.01	14.86
5000	8.88	12.52	18.58
6000	10.65	15.02	22.30
7500	13.31	18.78	27.87
10000	17.75	25.04	37.16
12500	22.19	31.30	46.45
15000	26.63	37.56	55.74
25000	44.38	62.59	92.90
40000	71.00	100.15	148.64
50000	88.75	125.18	185.80
75000	133.13	187.78	278.71
90000	159.75	225.33	334.45
100000	177.00	250.37	371.61